RESOURCE BOOKS FOR TEACHERS

series editor
ALAN MALEY

)UNG LEARNERS

Sarah Phillips

Oxford University Press

Oxford University Press
Great Clarendon Street, Oxford OX2 6DP

Oxford New York
Athens Auckland Bangkok Bogota Bombay
Buenos Aires Calcutta Cape Town Dar es Salaam Delhi
Florence Hong Kong Istanbul Karachi Kuala Lumpur
Madras Madrid Melbourne Mexico City Nairobi
Paris Singapore Taipei Tokyo Toronto

and associated companies in
Berlin Ibadan

Oxford and *Oxford English* are trade marks of
Oxford University Press

ISBN 0 19 437195 6

© Oxford University Press 1993

First published 1993
Fifth impression 1997

Photocopying

Set by Wyvern Typesetting, Bristol, UK

Printed in China

Acknowledgements

I would like to thank the many people who have, in one way or another, contributed to this book: readers, colleagues, teachers on courses, children I have taught, friends, and above all my parents John and Maria, and Angeles. Finally, I must thank Julia Sallabank, whose meticulous work on the manuscript has greatly added to the quality of the book.

The publisher and author would like to thank the following for their kind permission to use articles, extracts, or adaptations from copyright material. There might be instances where we have been unable to trace or contact the copyright holder before our printing deadline. We apologize for this and if notified the publisher will be pleased to rectify any errors or omissions at the earliest opportunity.

'Happy birthday to you' by Patty S. Hill and Mildred Hill © 1935 (renewed 1962), Summy Birchard Music, a division of Summy Birchard Inc., USA. All rights reserved. Reproduced by permission of Keith Prowse Music Pub. Co. Ltd., London WC2 0EA.

'Ten little fingers' by Pamela Conn Beall. Based on *Wee Sing*—*Children's Songs and Fingerplays* © 1977, 1985 by Pamela Conn Beall and Susan Hagen Nipp. Available from Price Stern Sloan, Inc. Publishers, Los Angeles, California.

'Five little elephants' by Yvonne Winer, from *Of Frogs and Snails*. Reproduced by kind permission of Belair Publications Ltd.

Illustrations by Oxford Illustrators Ltd., Ann Gowland, and Gwen Sallabank.

Contents

The author and series editor

Sarah Phillips trained as an English Language teacher at the Bell School, Norwich, and took her MSc in ELT at Edinburgh University. She has held various teaching posts in Europe, and is currently teaching at the Instituto de Idiomas at the University of Santiago de Compostela, Galicia, Spain. She also works with the Autonomous Government of Galicia on training courses and preparing materials for use in primary schools. She is also part of a Ministry of Education project developing materials for the first six years of English in school.

Alan Maley worked for The British Council from 1962 to 1988, serving as English Language Officer in Yugoslavia, Ghana, Italy, France, and China, and as Regional Representative for The British Council in South India (Madras). From 1988 to 1993 he was Director-General of the Bell Educational Trust, Cambridge. He is currently Senior Fellow in the Department of English Language and Literature of the National University of Singapore. His publications include *Quartet* (with Françoise Grellet and Wim Welsing, OUP 1982), *Literature*, in this series (with Alan Duff, OUP 1990), *Beyond Words*, *Sounds Interesting*, *Sounds Intriguing*, *Words*, *Variations on a Theme*, and *Drama Techniques in Language Learning* (all with Alan Duff), *The Mind's Eye* (with Françoise Grellet and Alan Duff), and *Learning to Listen* and *Poem into Poem* (with Sandra Moulding). He is also Series Editor for the Oxford Supplementary Skills series.

Foreword

Interest in the teaching of English to younger learners has been steadily growing in recent years. This is no doubt partly in response to the rapidly growing demand for it to be taught at even younger ages by parents who want to provide their children with a competitive educational advantage.

It has found expression in the large numbers of private language schools catering to this age-group which have sprung up in many parts of the world. Ministries of Education too have begun to respond, with large-scale expansion of provision for foreign language teaching at primary levels in countries such as France and Italy. The need for good materials is all the more pressing, given the minimal standards of many private schools, and the inadequate provision of trained teachers and suitable materials for the state systems. Yet the demand for English keeps on growing.

The growth of primary English has, moreover, had the effect of a 'shot in the arm' for the TEFL 'profession'. TEFL has tended to develop separately from the mainstream of educational thought and practice. There has, for example, been rather little cross-fertilization between TEFL and the teaching of other foreign languages. While this has undoubtedly enabled TEFL to develop some highly innovative and valuable practices and procedures of its own, ultimately such isolation is damaging and can lead to a comfortable parochialism.

The awakening of interest in teaching young learners offers TEFL one way back into the mainstream of education. Teachers of young learners need special skills, many of which have little to do with the language, which becomes a by-product of learning activities rather than a centrepiece. Helping the child to learn and develop becomes more important than simply teaching the language. The approach and techniques are therefore drawn from good general educational theory and practice rather than from a narrow TEFL repertoire.

Many EFL teachers wishing to enter the teaching of young learners will find the activities in this book an invaluable introduction, as will practising primary teachers wishing to move into TEFL. Experienced teachers will also find ideas they can develop further.

The teaching of young learners is immensely rewarding and exhilarating: children communicate a great sense of energy, curiosity, and involvement. This book will help teachers channel a sizeable part of this energy into productive learning.

Alan Maley

Introduction

Who this book is for

Young learners

In this book, 'young learners' means children from the first year
of formal schooling (five or six years old) to eleven or twelve
years of age. However, as any children's teacher will know, it is
not so much the children's age that counts in the classroom as
how mature they are. There are many factors that influence
children's maturity: for example, their culture, their environment
(city or rural), their sex, the expectations of their peers and
parents. The approach and type of activity that you decide to use
with a class will be influenced by your knowledge of their
circumstances, attitudes, and interests rather than simply by the
children's physical age. So although a recommended age range is
given for each activity, it should be taken as a guide, not a hard
and fast rule.

Their teachers

As English becomes more and more accepted as an international
language, it is increasingly included in primary curricula, where
it is often taught by non-native speakers. Although they are
trained primary teachers, they may not be trained language
teachers. There are also more and more private language schools
that provide classes for young learners: their teachers are often
native speakers who have not had specific training in teaching
children.

One of the aims of this book is to provide information and
activities that will meet the needs of these two very different
groups of teachers. I hope that there will be at least something
for everyone and that the second aim of this book, to provide
teachers with ideas and techniques that they can use when
designing supplementary activities for their own classes, will be
achieved.

Primary education

The years at primary school are extremely important in
children's intellectual, physical, emotional, and social

development. They go through a series of stages, progressively acquiring skills that are thought necessary by the society they live in. Many of these skills are interdependent, and if one has not been sufficiently developed, the acquisition of another may be impeded. For example, children who are unable to identify the odd shape in the following group will have difficulty in differentiating between the letters *p*, *b*, and *d*.

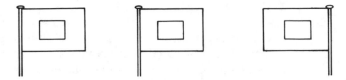

Similarly, if an older child is unable to dissociate him- or herself from the here and now, and to project and enter into imaginary or hypothetical worlds, he or she will find it difficult to make deductions from evidence, to apply his or her experience to other situations, or indeed to accept that the world has not always been as it is now. This is a serious handicap in educational systems in which knowledge is usually acquired from books and not from firsthand experience.

On the physical side, children need to develop balance, spatial awareness, and fine control of certain muscles in order to play sports and perform everyday actions such as dressing themselves, cleaning their teeth, colouring, drawing, and writing.

Socially, children need to develop a series of characteristics to enable them to fit into the society they live in, to become aware of themselves in relation to others, to share and co-operate, and to be assertive without being aggressive. These social skills vary from culture to culture and generation to generation and often form part of the 'hidden curriculum', although they are increasingly being defined by Ministries of Education.

Finally, it is increasingly recognized that children need to 'learn how to learn'. This means that their education and learning should not be confined to the limits of their classroom, textbooks, and teacher, but that we should help them to acquire skills and independence that will enable them to continue learning outside and beyond school. This implies that they need to be able to accept criticism and become self-critical, to be aware of how they learn, and to experiment with different learning styles, to organize their work, and to be open and interested in all that surrounds them.

All this means that primary language teachers have a much wider responsibility than the mere teaching of a language system: they need to bear in mind the education of the whole child when planning their teaching programme.

Teaching English as a Foreign Language to young learners

The way children learn a foreign language, and therefore the way to teach it, obviously depends on their developmental stage. It would not be reasonable to ask a child to do a task that demands a sophisticated control of spatial orientation (for example, tracing a route on a map) if he or she has not yet developed this skill. On the other hand, beginners of 11 or 12 years of age will not respond well to an activity that they perceive as childish, or well below their intellectual level, even if it is linguistically appropriate (for example, identifying an odd shape out or matching picture halves).

As a general rule, it can be assumed that the younger the children are, the more holistic learners they will be. Younger learners respond to language according to what it does or what they can do with it, rather than treating it as an intellectual game or abstract system. This has both advantages and disadvantages: on the one hand they respond to the meaning underlying the language used and do not worry about individual words or sentences; on the other, they do not make the analytical links that older learners do. Younger learners have the advantage of being great mimics, are often unselfconscious, and are usually prepared to enjoy the activities the teacher has prepared for them. These factors mean that it is easy to maintain a high degree of motivation and to make the English class an enjoyable, stimulating experience for the children. Here are some points to bear in mind:

- The activities should be simple enough for the children to understand what is expected of them.
- The task should be within their abilities: it needs to be achievable but at the same time sufficiently stimulating for them to feel satisfied with their work.
- The activities should be largely orally based—indeed, with very young children listening activities will take up a large proportion of class time.
- Written activities should be used sparingly with younger children. Children of six or seven years old are often not yet proficient in the mechanics of writing in their own language.

The kinds of activities that work well are games and songs with actions, total physical response activities, tasks that involve colouring, cutting, and sticking, simple, repetitive stories, and simple, repetitive speaking activities that have an obvious communicative value.

As children mature they bring more intellectual, motor, and social skills to the classroom, as well as a wider knowledge of the world. All these can be applied to the process of acquiring another language. The wider resources of older children should be exploited to the full while maintaining the philosophy of making a language relevant, practical, and communicative. This means the development of all the four skills, and the use of a wide range of topics that could well draw on other subjects in the curriculum. The focus should continue to be on language as a vehicle of communication and not on the grammar, though the ability of older children to make logical links and deductions can be exploited. You can give them tasks in which they discover for themselves simple grammatical rules, or you can focus their attention on the structure of the language in order to help them formulate an 'internal grammar' of their own. This is part of the 'learning to learn' process mentioned above.

It is common sense that if an activity is enjoyable, it will be memorable; the language involved will 'stick', and the children will have a sense of achievement which will develop motivation for further learning. This cyclical process generates a positive attitude towards learning English, which is perhaps one of the most valuable things that primary teachers can transmit to children. Children learn at lot more than English in their English classes: the tasks and activities stimulate and continue their all-round development.

In the classroom

Which language to use in class?

The question of whether or not to use the mother tongue in the English classroom is an open one. My own feeling is that while it is essential to use as much English as possible in class, there are times when the use of English is counter-productive. It is often more economical and less frustrating for all concerned if you give instructions for a complicated activity in the children's mother tongue, or check the instructions you have given by asking the children to repeat them in their own language. In a feedback session (see below), where the aim is for the children to express their feelings and attitudes, it would be counter-productive to expect them to use their limited knowledge of English. What is important is that the children are given clear guidelines on when they are expected to use English and when their first language is permissible. Children need to be aware of which activities are specifically intended to develop their spoken skills; they should be encouraged to use only English in these. On the other hand, if they are working on a reading text that requires logical inference, it is not reasonable to expect them to be able to do this in English.

Classroom language

An area where English should be used as much as possible is the everyday organization and running of the classroom. Both the teacher and the children can use English here; in fact, this classroom language is one of the most realistic communicative situations in which the children find themselves. It is not difficult to give instructions for the usual classroom routines in English: if you use gestures as well, the children will soon become used to them.

If you have been working on requests or asking permission using *can*, then you should insist that the children make simple requests such as *Can I have a pencil?* or *Can we start?* in English. One way of encouraging the use of English in the classroom is to write the most commonly used phrases in speech bubbles and to stick them where the children can see them clearly. If a child uses his or her mother tongue, do not respond to the request, but insist that he or she repeats it in English by pointing to the appropriate bubble.

Classroom organization

The children

Different activities require different groupings. The ones most commonly used are:

individual: for reading, making things, or keeping vocabulary records.

pairs: pair work is most commonly used in speaking activities like mini role plays or information gaps, and you can also ask the children to read and write in pairs. When you are setting up such an activity, it is a good idea to demonstrate what you want the children to do using 'open pairs'. Select two children to do part of the activity while the rest of the class watches.

groups: groups consist of three or more children: it is usually counter-productive to have groups of more than five.

whole class: the children may work as a whole class focused on the teacher, for example in a presentation or game, or as a whole class with the teacher acting as a monitor, for example in a mingling activity such as 'Find your partner' (in 2.1, 'Simple speaking activities').

Working in groups may be new to the children and they may at first find it difficult, as children need time to develop the ability to take responsibility and work without constant supervision. If this is the case, start with pairs and tightly controlled activities, and gradually introduce larger groups and freer activities.

Tables and chairs

The physical organization of the classroom is important. In an ideal world the classroom would have an area of easily movable desks and chairs, an open space for action songs and games, a quiet corner for reading or self-study, and a table and notice-board where the children's work can be displayed. Such ideal conditions are rarely found in the real world, but if at all possible arrange the tables and chairs so that the children can work in pairs or groups, and there is a space for children to come out to the board and to move around the classroom. Often the five or ten minutes spent on reorganizing tables and chairs are well worth it to help an activity work well.

Display

Many of the activities in this book have a 'final product', for example a picture, a graph, a book, or models. A corner of the classroom or an 'English' section of the classroom wall where the children's work is displayed encourages the children to take a pride and interest in what they do. For some good ideas on display, see *Bright Ideas Display* by Rhona Whiteford and Jim Fitzsimmons (see the Further Reading section at the end of this book for details).

Notebooks and folders

Children need to be shown how to organize their work. By doing this you can help the children to take a pride in their work and to understand and to participate in the underlying organization of their notes. One way is to have a folder divided by topics in which they keep all their worksheets, grammar, and vocabulary notes. Alternatively, each child could keep a separate vocabulary notebook which will grow year by year. You may like to introduce a system where each week a group of children summarizes the week's work on a poster on the 'English wall'. Whatever the system, it is vital that it is consistent, and that you set aside time for it in class. Younger children need much more supervision, while older children should be encouraged to be responsible for their own work.

Feedback

Feedback is an important, even vital, part of the language learning process. Feedback is a time in class when the children and teacher can look back at, and reflect on, what they have been doing. It can be thought of as a kind of breathing space, a quiet time before going on to the next activity or language area.

There are two kinds of feedback, which focus on: (1) the language you have been working on, and (2) the way the children have achieved the task, and on their behaviour, both as individuals and as a group.

Feedback can take place immediately after the children have done an activity, or at the end of a series of activities, or on a fixed day each week or fortnight—in fact at any time that the teacher feels it will be useful. What is important is that feedback is a regular feature of lessons, allowing the children and teacher to develop insights into themselves and their learning and to build an overview of their language learning progress.

A few ways of conducting feedback are outlined below. One thing they have in common is that the role of the teacher is not to dominate, but to listen and interpret what the children are saying in a more concise and coherent form. The feedback session is an opportunity for the children to contribute their thoughts, feelings, and ideas to the class. This handing over of control is not an easy step for the teacher to take, and the children find the idea a bit strange at first too, so it is best to start with very simple activities in order to establish the concept. Feedback should be done in the children's native language, as the aim is not to practise English, but to involve the children in the learning process.

Some ideas for conducting feedback:

– At the end of an activity, ask the children to show what they thought of it by drawing a face which reflects how they feel about the activity.

Discuss the results with the children, and bear in mind the activities they like when planning the next unit of work.

- As in the previous activity, but ask the children to evaluate the activity on two scales—'useful' and 'interesting'.

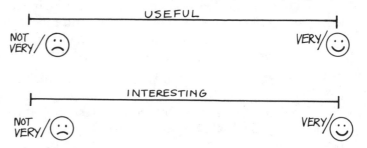

- Ask the children to look through their folders and to think back over the class, and to write down five useful pieces of language that they have learned.

- Ask the children to look through their folders and to write down five things that they have learned—language or other things.

- At the end of a unit of work, ask older children to write you a letter or note in which they mention the things they have enjoyed doing and the things they do not understand.

- Ask the children to write sentences such as these on a regular basis:

  I am good at ...
  I am not good at ...
  I am going to ... next week.

- At the end of a group or whole class activity, ask the children to decide where they would put their corporate behaviour on the following (or similar) scale:

VERY GOOD   VERY BAD

Then ask them where they think you would put them. If there is a difference, and there usually is, ask them why. If the evaluation is towards the 'very bad' end of the scale, ask them how they could improve. This is made much more explicit if you use a wall of the classroom as the scale, and ask the children to literally put themselves on it.

— After a group activity, ask each group to write four or five pieces of advice for another group that is going to do the same activity. This could take the form of simple imperatives:

Remember to ...
Don't ....

This is especially useful if you are going to repeat the type of activity. Before doing it again, remind the children of their ideas.

— After an activity that has required the application of logic, reasoning, or a skill of some kind, ask the children how they have reached their answers. This can help those who had problems with the activity, giving them ideas or a model for how to do better.

— Ask the children to keep a graph of their English classes: they can enter their progress according to 'I worked', 'I learned', or any other parameters that you or they think useful.

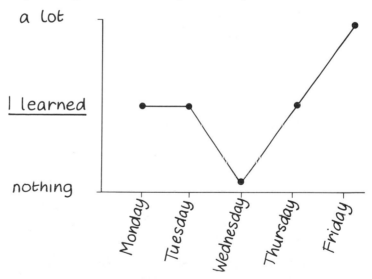

As you get used to doing feedback, you will think of other ways of getting your children to reflect on themselves and their lessons. You may be surprised at the children's capacity to be self-critical, and their awareness of the teacher's aims and of their own learning processes. This kind of reflection is starting to appear in textbooks such as *Hotline* by Tom Hutchinson (OUP): they are worth looking through for ideas, even though they are written for older children.

A final word

Teaching children is tremendously rewarding. The time spent on preparing classes that reflect their interests and needs is time well spent, as, perhaps more than with any other group of learners, children respond wholeheartedly to your efforts. They know instinctively whether you enjoy working with them and whether your lessons are thoughtfully prepared: if so, the children will respond with a similar effort. Groups of children absorbed in a task or a display, the nerves and excitement that accompany a class performance, or a thoughtful piece of reflection, are all signs that a class is working well, both on the part of the children and their teacher. I hope you will find some ideas in this book to contribute to a fruitful language classroom.

How to use this book

How the book is organized

The book is divided into ten chapters. The first five focus on the four language skills, and grammar and vocabulary; then there are four chapters on techniques which are especially useful in the primary classroom. The last chapter shows how the activities can be put together to form a unit of work. Most of the activities have a topic focus so that you can integrate them with the activities in your textbook; alternatively, you can use the techniques to make your own activities suitable for your particular classes. To help you find the activity you want, there is an index at the back of the book, which as well as grammar and vocabulary topics, shows you whether the activity links with other subjects in the school curriculum such as mathematics, drama, or story-telling, and whether it practises 'life skills' such as co-operation and observation. There is also a comprehensive Further Reading section.

How each activity is organized

The organization is as follows:

Level
1 = beginners: from children with little or no knowledge of English, to those who recognize the English names of colours, numbers up to twelve, and basic vocabulary such as the family, animals, some food, *I am/you are, there is/there are, can, I like/don't like*, and classroom commands such as *stand up*, *sit down, open your books*. Their active use of this language will be very limited.
2 = elementary: These children are able to use level 1 language more actively, and to make simple sentences and questions. They will have a wider range of vocabulary: for example, clothes, shops, parts of the body, verbs for daily routines, and telling the time in English (if they know this in their own language).
3 = pre-intermediate: These children will be more capable of recognizing sentence patterns and generating language of their own. They are ready to learn structures such as the past simple, comparatives, possibly *going to*, and functions such as obligation, requests, or making suggestions.

It is very important not to confuse these levels with years of

English, as a child's maturity makes a great difference to what he or she is able to do. An older child may reach level 2 in one year, while younger children need to go more slowly.

Age group
The letters A, B, and C refer to children's ages:
A = 6–8 years old
B = 8–10 years old
C = 10–12 years old.

This is a rough guide only. You must, of course, use your own knowledge of your children to judge whether the activity is suitable for your class (see 'Who this book is for', page 5).

Time
A rough guide to how long the activity will take. This will vary considerably according to such factors as the size of the class, the age of the children, whether they are used to working in groups, and so on.

Aims
The aims of the activity are divided into two parts: linguistic aims and 'other' aims. The linguistic aims cover language and skills development, while the other aims refer to the intellectual and social development of the children.

Description
A short summary of the activity so that you can get an overall idea of it.

Materials
A list of what you need to do the activity.

Preparation
A brief outline of what you need to do before the lesson.

In class
A step-by-step guide to doing the activity.

One of the first steps is often 'Check the vocabulary/language'. The amount of checking will depend on the needs of each group: teachers may need to take time to present and practise the language, or simply to remind the children of it.

After doing the activities it is important to give the children time to take a step back and to reflect on what they have done—see the section on feedback, page 11.

Follow-up
Ideas for further activities which reinforce what has been learned.

Variations
Examples of ways in which you could adapt the activity to suit your children.

Comments
Hints and advice to make the activity run more smoothly.

1 Listening

Listening tasks are extremely important in the primary language classroom, providing a rich source of language data from which the children begin to build up their own idea of how the language works. This knowledge forms a base or resource which they will eventually draw on in order to produce language themselves. Let the children listen to language which is a little above the level with which they are already familiar. Make the meaning clear by using pictures, mime, and body language, and they will understand it and expand their language horizons just a little bit further.

It is almost always true that language learners understand more than they can say, and when children learn their first language they respond to language long before they learn to speak. Second language learners also have a 'silent period' in which they listen to the language around them, internalize it, and formulate their own personal grammar, which they adapt and expand as they are exposed to more language. Some authors argue that this period should be respected and that students learning a new language should not be made to speak (or write) until they are ready, that is, until they do so spontaneously. Many of the activities in this chapter require children to respond non-verbally, or using a minimum of language. This allows them to focus on what they are listening to and to demonstrate that they have understood it, without being distracted by how to formulate their answer. The exception to this is written dictation, which requires children to produce at least some writing.

There is a tendency to think that 'doing listening' is listening to the cassette that comes with the coursebook. Cassettes are useful for providing a different voice and accent, but the teacher is also a very important source of listening material. When, as a teacher, you go about the daily business of organizing the class, you provide some truly authentic listening material (a good reason for giving as many classroom instructions as you can in English). Teachers can also give instructions for making things (see 1.6, 'Make an instructions machine'), or tell stories (see 1.2, 'The Frog family'), and because you are actually there in the classroom the children can see your face, gestures, and body language, which help them understand. You are also able to interact with the children while they listen, which is after all how we listen in real life. Don't underestimate yourself!

Stories

Stories are a feature of all cultures and have a universal appeal. Stories in the broadest sense (including anecdotes, jokes, 'you'll never guess what happened to me', etc.) fascinate both children and adults—everybody loves a story—and they can be used to great effect in the language classroom. You can find stories everywhere—one brainstorming session I had with a group of teachers came up with all these sources for stories:

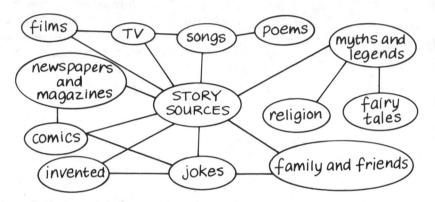

If a story is to be successful, never read it, tell it! In order to do this:

1 Prepare yourself an outline or skeleton of the story which contains the main points.

2 Practise telling the story out loud, perhaps to a friend or colleague, or into a tape recorder.

3 Remember to use expression, mime, and gestures. (Practise in front of a mirror!)

4 Remember to keep eye contact with the people you are telling the story to.

5 Don't rush it, enjoy it.

When you have told your story there are lots of things you can do with it, for example:

- Give the children sentences that tell the story out of order and ask them to put them in the right order
- In groups, give each child a picture of part of the story. The children describe their pictures to each other and put them in order
- Give the children the story in split sentences and ask them to match the halves
- Give the children a gapped version of the story and ask them to fill in the gaps
- Get the children to dramatize the story, perhaps with puppets
- Get the children to mime the story as you tell it
- Get the children to draw a comic strip of the story.

Further storytelling ideas are contained in this chapter (for example, 1.2, 'The Frog family', and 1.3, 'Timmy goes shopping—Listen and identify'), and in later chapters (for example, 8.1, 'Milly and Molly and the Big, Bad Cat'); and also in *Once Upon a Time* by Morgan and Rinvolucri (see the Further Reading section).

Total Physical Response

Several of the ideas in this chapter incorporate techniques based on Total Physical Response (TPR). This is an extremely useful and adaptable teaching technique, especially in primary classes. With TPR the children listen to their teacher telling them what to do, and then do it. Instructions can range from something as simple as *Touch your nose* to more complex sentences like *Go and stand next to the girl who's wearing a red jumper, but who isn't wearing black shoes.* Children, especially very young ones, are able to understand much, much more than they can produce, and this technique builds on that capacity.

Many of the listening activities in this chapter are of the 'listen and respond' type: Activity 1.1, 'Listen and do', suggests some standard TPR activities, while 1.2, 'The Frog family', shows how the technique can be extended to story telling, and 1.6, 'Make an instructions machine', extends it to paper folding. Other activities which involve a certain amount of TPR include 1.4, 'Complete a grid', and 1.5, 'The Pied Piper'.

1.1 Listen and do: TPR activities

LEVEL	**All**
AGE GROUP	**All**
TIME	**10 minutes +**
AIMS	**Linguistic:** intensive listening skills, to develop 'intuitive' listening, to present and practise structures and vocabulary. **Other:** physical co-ordination; acting skills.
DESCRIPTION	The children listen to their teacher giving instructions and obey them.
MATERIALS	Usually none, though in some activities it is useful to bring in things to show the children.

PREPARATION   Prepare a list of commands related to the topic or language
point that you are working on. Here are some examples:

Suggestions for TPR

Classroom commands (adapt these to your own routine)	Stand up. Sit down. Give X a pencil, please. Open/close the door. Put up your hand.
Body	Touch your partner's back. Put your hand on your head. Hold up seven fingers.
Verbs in general (mime)	Eat an orange. Drink a very cold fizzy drink. Go to the shop and ask for some chewing gum. Watch a horror film.
Prepositions	Put your pencil on the floor. Put your book under the chair.
Abilities	If you can swim, clap once. If you can play the recorder, stand up.
Physical descriptions	Hold hands with someone with brown eyes. Touch someone who is wearing a red jumper.
Comparatives	If Y is taller than Z, put up your left hand. If my chair is bigger than yours, clap your hands twice.
Likes and dislikes	If you like bananas, pretend you are eating one. If you don't like eggs, make a face.
General knowledge (These can reflect topics the children are working on.)	If London is the capital of England, put up your hand. If ice is made from water, nod your head. If a spider has eight legs, clap eight times.

IN CLASS	Start with simple commands and build up to more complicated ones. It is usually not necessary to pre-teach vocabulary; instead, demonstrate or let the children try and guess what you want them to do. You can ask the whole class to respond to a command, or single out one child at a time.
VARIATION	This is a version of a traditional children's game called 'Simon says'.

1 When you say *Teacher says* before a command, the children have to obey it. If you do not say *Teacher says*, the children mustn't move.

2 Children who move when you don't say 'Teacher says' are 'out', and help you watch the others for the rest of the game. The winners are the last ones left at the end of the game.

1.2 The Frog family

LEVEL	1
AGE GROUP	A, B
TIME	30 minutes
AIMS	**Linguistic:** listening for gist, relating words and actions, family vocabulary. **Other:** to involve the children in storytelling.
DESCRIPTION	The teacher tells a story about the Frog family and the children act out the parts of the characters.
MATERIALS	Flashcards or board drawings of the Frog family, chalk or string, paper for lily-pads.
PREPARATION	**1** Practise telling the story. Include very explicit actions that the children will be able to imitate.

2 Prepare pictures of the Frog family.

3 Draw a large lily-pad and make an area of floor into a 'pond' with chalk or string.

IN CLASS

1 Tell the children in their first language that you are going to tell them a story about the Frog family and either draw the frogs or put up pictures on the board. Check that they know who is who.

2 Ask the children questions like: 'Have you ever seen a frog?' 'Where do frogs live?' 'What do they sit on?' 'Do they like to be hot or cold?' and 'How can they get cool?' Then show them the outline of the pond on the floor and the big lily-pad in it.

3 Tell them the story, remembering to use lots of gestures to make the meaning very clear.

4 Tell the children you are going to tell the story again, but this time five of them are going to be the Frog family. Ask for volunteers and line them up by the edge of the pond.

5 Tell the story again, and as each child hears their character they put up their hand. Encourage them to do the gestures with you as you tell the story.

6 All the children will want to have a go at acting out the story: once they have heard it several times you can divide the class into several 'ponds' and tell the story with several Frog families at a time.

STORY OUTLINE

This is the most basic version of the story. You can add details like names and sizes if you want to, though they should always be things that you can illustrate with mime or pictures.

THE FROG FAMILY

Story	Actions
This is a story about Daddy frog, Mummy frog, Sister frog, Brother frog, and Baby frog.	*Point to the pictures as you name the frogs.*
It was hot—very, very hot,	*Wipe your forehead, and make 'hot' gestures.*
and Daddy frog	*Point to the picture of Daddy frog and squat down beside the pond.*
went jump, jump, jump, and sat on a leaf in the pond.	*Jump three times and sit on the leaf in the pond.*
Mummy frog was hot—very, very hot.	*Point to Mummy frog, squat by the pond, and make 'hot' gestures.*
So Daddy frog said 'Come here!'	*Point to Daddy frog, return to the leaf, and beckon to Mummy frog.*
Mummy frog went jump, jump, jump, and sat on the leaf in the pond.	*Point to Mummy frog, squat by the pond, and jump three times to sit on the leaf by Daddy frog.*

Sister frog was hot—very, very hot.	*Point to Sister frog, squat by the pond, and make 'hot' gestures.*
So Mummy frog said 'Come here!'	*Point to Mummy frog, return to the leaf, and beckon to Sister frog.*
Sister frog went jump, jump, jump, and sat on the leaf in the pond.	*Point to sister frog, squat by the pond, and jump three times to sit on the leaf by Mummy frog.*
Brother frog was hot—very, very hot.	*Point to Brother frog, squat by the pond, and make 'hot' gestures.*
So Sister frog said 'Come here!'	*Point to Sister frog, return to the leaf, and beckon to Brother frog.*
Brother frog went jump, jump, jump, and	*Point to Brother frog, squat by the pond, and jump three times to sit on the leaf by Sister frog.*
Baby frog was hot—very, very hot.	*Point to Baby frog, squat by the pond, and make 'hot' gestures.*
So Brother frog said 'Come here!'	*Point to Brother frog, return to the leaf, and beckon to Baby frog.*
Baby frog went jump, jump, jump, and sat on the leaf in the pond.	*Point to Baby frog, squat by the pond, and jump three times to sit on the leaf by Brother frog.*
And then—SPLASH—they all fell into the water!	*Start to move backwards and forwards as if you were losing your balance and fall into the pond.*

FOLLOW-UP 1   Ask the children to draw a picture of the Frog family.

FOLLOW-UP 2   The children can make masks for the characters as a 'Read and make' activity (see 8.9, 'Making masks').

1.3 Timmy goes shopping—listen and identify

LEVEL   2

AGE GROUP   A, B

TIME   30 minutes

AIMS   **Linguistic:** listening for detail, the language of shops and shopping, to give passive exposure to verbs in the past simple tense, to relate speech to pictures.

DESCRIPTION	The children listen to a story and choose pictures that fit what they have heard.
MATERIALS	Examples of food, for example fruit, sausages, and bread, or pictures of these. Pictures of shopping baskets (see Preparation).
PREPARATION	1 Make a photocopy of the four different shopping baskets for each child (see Worksheet 1.3 at the end of the book), or make four large pictures of the baskets that you can stick on the board.
	2 Practise telling the story using the story outline below. Remember to use plenty of gestures, mime, and pictures to help the children understand.
IN CLASS	1 Tell the children you are going to tell them the story of a boy called Timmy who went shopping.
	2 Ask them 'Do you ever go shopping? Do you go on your own? Or do you go with Mummy or Daddy?'
	3 Show them the food (or pictures) and ask them in which shop you buy what. Teach the English names of the shops and write them on the board. If you are using pictures of food, you can stick them next to the names.
	4 Ask the children if they have a list of things to buy when they go shopping. Draw one on the board. Ask the children to suggest things to buy. Then wipe these items off so that you have an empty list.
	5 Tell the story. (See the story outline below.)
	6 Then ask the children to tell you what was on Timmy's shopping list and which shops he went to. Write these on the board.
	7 Give the children the pictures of the baskets (or put the large pictures on the board) and tell them that one of them is Timmy's basket when he got home.
	8 Tell the story again.
	9 Ask the children to discuss in pairs which is Timmy's basket, then ask the whole class which basket they chose and why. (This will probably be done in their native language, which is fine as this activity is designed to practise listening comprehension, not speaking in English.)

STORY OUTLINE

TIMMY GOES SHOPPING

One day Timmy's mother asked him to go to the shops. She gave him a shopping list.

On the list were:
two loaves of bread,
twelve sausages,
five apples,
and six fat fish.

He went to the baker's and bought two loaves of bread.

went—butcher's—bought twelve sausages

went—fruit shop—bought five apples

went—fish shop—bought six fat fish.

On the way home he met a duck who said 'I'm hungry', so Timmy gave her a loaf of bread.

met a dog—said 'I'm hungry'—gave him six sausages

met a donkey—said 'I'm hungry'—gave her three apples

met a cat—said 'I'm hungry'—gave him a fish.

He got home and put the shopping basket on the table.

His mother said:

'Oh Timmy! I said two loaves, not one
twelve sausages, not six
five apples, not two
six fish, not five.

Next time we'll go together!'

COMMENTS

The food and shops should reflect the children's environment—the example given here is for children who live in southern Europe.

FOLLOW-UP 1

1 Tell the story again, but change the name of the child and the numbers of items to fit a different basket on the picture.

2 Ask the children which is the correct basket.

FOLLOW-UP 2

Tell the story again, but ask the children to give you different details.

FOLLOW-UP 3

1 Draw a cartoon strip of the story with empty speech bubbles.

2 Make copies and give them to the children. Ask them to complete the speech bubbles.

You can either let them make up their own words, or give them sentences that they have to match to the correct speech bubble.

FOLLOW-UP 4

The children act out the story. If their English is limited, give each child a role and get them to come to the front and mime the story as you tell it. If they know more English they can say the words spoken by the characters.

1.4 Complete a grid

LEVEL

All

AGE GROUP

A, B

TIME

20 minutes

AIMS

Linguistic: recognizing the English names of letters, numbers, and colours.
Other: to practise using a grid, spatial awareness.

DESCRIPTION

The children make a picture by listening to the teacher and colouring squares on a grid.

MATERIALS

A large piece of paper for the teacher, copies of empty grids for the children, coloured pencils, and chalk.

PREPARATION

1 Draw a grid like the one illustrated below, if possible on a large piece of paper so that the children can see it clearly.

2 Write the numbers and letters you want to practise along the sides. These could simply be 1–10 and A–J, or you might want to practise problematic numbers and letters, for example, 13 and 30, 14 and 40, or E, I, C, and S.

3 Make a copy of an empty grid for each child.

4 Use your grid to make a simple coloured picture, either using one of the examples below, or one that fits the topic you are working on.

EXAMPLES

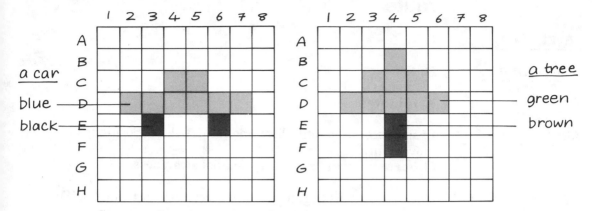

IN CLASS

1 Draw a large grid on the board and write along the sides of it the numbers and letters you have chosen to practise.

2 Say the number and letter of one square and then invite a child to come to the board to show the square you are referring to. Say a colour, and let him or her choose the chalk to colour the square. For example: A3, red.

Do this a few times until the children have got the idea of the grid and you have built up a simple picture.

3 Tell the children that they are all going to make a picture like this.

4 Give out the empty grids and ask them to copy the numbers and letters from the board. If you have no photocopier, they will have to draw their own grids or use squared paper.

5 Call out the letters, numbers, and colours of the squares in your picture, marking off the squares you have said on your master copy. You will probably need to say all the squares two or three times to let the slower ones catch up and so that all the children can check their work.

6 Ask the children what the picture shows. Then show them your master picture so they can see if they got it right.

FOLLOW-UP

The children can make up their own pictures and dictate them to one another—warn them to make them simple! If you are studying a topic, get them to draw something connected with the topic. You can display the pictures as a vocabulary poster.

1.5 The Pied Piper—listen and draw a route

LEVEL	2, 3
AGE GROUP	B, C
TIME	30 minutes
AIMS	**Linguistic:** to practise listening for detail, prepositions of movement. **Other:** to practise map skills, spatial awareness.
DESCRIPTION	The teacher tells the story of the Pied Piper of Hamelin. The children listen and draw where he led the rats on a map.
PREPARATION	1 Make two copies of the map for yourself, and a copy of the map for each child (see Worksheet 1.5 at the end of the book). 2 Draw the route on one of your copies of the map. Leave the other one blank to show the children. 3 Practise telling the story.
IN CLASS	1 Show the children a picture of a tall man with a flute and lots of rats. Ask the children if they know who he is.

2 Tell the story of the Pied Piper (see story outline below).

3 Give the children their copies of the map and check that they understand the English for the main features (*bridge, hill, castle, road, house, wood, river*). You can ask them to write the words on their own maps.

4 Explain that you are going to tell them where the Pied Piper took the rats, and that they must draw it on the map.

5 Describe the route in English, once before they start to draw, so that they get a general idea, then again a couple of times while they are drawing.

6 Let them compare their routes, then describe the route once again, and finally show them your master copy so that they can check their work.

STORY OUTLINE

THE PIED PIPER

Once upon a time there was a town called Hamelin.

The people in the town had a problem: the town was full of rats! There were rats in the street, in the houses, in the schools, in the shops, even in their beds!

'We must get rid of the rats!' the people said. But how?

Then, one day, a strange man came to the town. He wore a tall hat and had a flute. 'I can get rid of the rats', he said. 'What will you give me if I take them all away?'

'Lots of money!' said the people.

So the Pied Piper started to play his flute. Strange music came out of the flute, and soon rats came out of all the shops, houses, and schools. The road was full of rats! They all followed the Pied Piper.

The Pied Piper led the rats:

over the bridge,
up the hill,
down the hill,
round the castle,
along the road,
past the little house,
through the garden of the big house,
into the wood,
out of the wood,
and into the river.

FOLLOW-UP 1

Give the children sentences from the story with words missing. They have to look at their maps to guess the missing words.

FOLLOW-UP 2	Ask the children to make up their own routes and describe them to each other.
FOLLOW-UP 3	Move the classroom furniture to represent the map and get the children to act out the route as you tell the story.
FOLLOW-UP 4	Tell the rest of the story—for sources see the Further Reading section.
COMMENTS	Remember that you can make this activity easier or more difficult by using more or less complicated language. To make it easier you can repeat words or sentences, or to make it more difficult you can add details that are not necessary for drawing the route, such as 'and there were brown rats and black rats and big rats and small rats'—the children have to listen harder.

1.6 Make an instructions machine

LEVEL	2, 3
AGE GROUP	B, C
TIME	**40 minutes**
AIMS	**Linguistic:** adverbs, questions, following spoken instructions. **Other:** to develop manual dexterity.
DESCRIPTION	The teacher shows the children how to fold paper to make a simple model that can be used to give instructions (or tell fortunes).
MATERIALS	Cards with action words and adverbs on (see Preparation), an 'instructions machine' which you have made (see below for how to do this), and a copy of Worksheet 1.6 (see back of book), scissors, and coloured pens or pencils for each child.
PREPARATION	1 Practise making the 'instructions machine' yourself, and then practise making it at the same time as saying how to make it.
	2 Make some small cards with these words on them: *jump, hop, skip, dance, quickly, slowly, loudly, quietly.*
IN CLASS	**Part One**
	This introduces the idea of instructions.

1 Write the words on the board, and check that the children know them.

2 Put the cards in two piles: verbs and adverbs. Take one card from each pile so that you have one verb and one adverb, and ask the children to do the action: for example, *jump quickly*, or *sing loudly*.

3 Then ask for a volunteer to take a card from each pile. They should not say what is on them out loud, but do the action.

4 The class has to guess which words he or she has got.

Part Two

5 Show the class the 'instructions machine' you have made and show them how it works. Tell them they are going to make one themselves. They will need to clear their desks and have coloured pencils ready.

6 Give out Worksheet 1.6. Tell them how to make the 'instructions machine', stage by stage, using the instructions below, demonstrating as you go. Do not go on to the next stage until everybody has finished the previous one! At Stage 3, use the words on the board to make up instructions to write in the 'machines'.

7 Let them play with their 'instructions machines'.

HOW TO MAKE AN INSTRUCTIONS MACHINE

1 Find the squares on the corners of the sheet of paper. Write in them *What's your name?*, *How old are you?*, *Where do you live?*, and *What's your favourite colour?*
(Pause)

How old are you?

2 Find the circles. Colour them red, orange, yellow, green, blue, purple, black, and brown.
(Pause)

3 Now find the empty triangles. Write an instruction in each of them.
(Pause)

4 Now turn the paper over.
(Pause)

5 Now fold the square in half along both diagonals and open it again. (Pause)

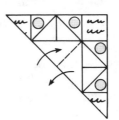 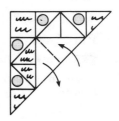 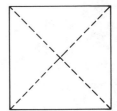

6 Now fold each corner to the middle. (Pause)

7 Turn it over.
(Pause)

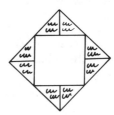

8 Fold the new corners to the middle. (Pause)

9 Fold it in half and open it again. (Pause)

10 Fold it in half the other way and open it again.
(Pause)

11 Now—the difficult part—put your finger and thumb in the flaps in the corners, and push upwards and to the middle.

The instructions machine works like this. Working with a partner:

1 Ask your partner to choose a question. If the question is How old are you?, open and close the machine once for each year of their age. If the question is What's your name?, Where do you live?, or What's your favourite colour?, spell the answer out loud and open and close the machine once for each letter.

2 Ask your partner to choose another question. Do the same thing with the answer.

3 Open the machine to the coloured flaps and ask your partner to choose one of the colours. Open the flap of this colour and your partner has to follow the instructions under the flap.

FOLLOW-UP

Ask the children what other instructions they could put in the machine. Show them how to make correct sentences and then let them make another machine with these in.

VARIATION 1

Instead of instructions, write predictions to make a fortune-telling machine.

VARIATION 2

Give instructions to make other simple folded paper figures, to go with topics you are working on: for example, if you are working on animals, make a zoo or Noah's ark. (See under 'Creative activities' in the Further Reading section for examples of books on paper folding.)

1.7 The teacher is a cassette player

LEVEL	2, 3
AGE GROUP	B, C
TIME	**20 minutes**
AIMS	**Linguistic:** listening and writing. **Other:** to encourage a sense of responsibility among the children.
DESCRIPTION	This is a dictation with a difference: the teacher acts as a 'cassette player' which responds to spoken commands.
PREPARATION	Choose a short text to work with, perhaps from your coursebook.
IN CLASS	1 Ask the children what buttons you find on a cassette player. As they tell you, write the English names on the board like this:

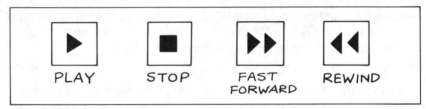

2 Tell the children that you are going to give them a dictation that is rather unusual. Explain that you are a cassette player and that when they say the commands on the board, you do what they say. They have to write down what the 'cassette player' says. The 'cassette player' cannot do anything without a command in English. Check that the children understand by asking 'What do you say to make me start?'

3 Say 'Right, we're ready to start' and wait until someone says *Play.*

4 Start to read the text at a normal speaking pace and keep going until someone (usually in desperation!) says *Stop.*

At first it will probably be chaotic: be patient, and resist the temptation to interfere, to speak more slowly, or to stop—it is very important for the success of the activity that you are a 'machine' that only obeys their commands.

5 Carry on like this to the end of the text.

6 When they have finished, ask them to check what they have written in pairs and to look for mistakes. Then go through the text with the whole class.

FOLLOW-UP   This is an activity where feedback (see Introduction, page 11) can be very fruitful as it gives the children a chance to reflect on what they have done. Ask them if they liked the activity. Why? Why not? How could they do it better next time? Write down what they say, and the next time you do this kind of dictation, get them to remember their comments before you start.

COMMENTS   This dictation has the advantage of handing the control over to the children. They can go back and forwards as often as they like. It is important to remember that a cassette player has no mind of its own and no speed control, and that the speed of the dictation should be a normal talking pace.

1.8 In the playground—a picture dictation

LEVEL   2

AGE GROUP   All

TIME   20–30 minutes

AIMS   **Linguistic:** vocabulary (actions), prepositions, the present continuous, *there is*, *there are*, listening for detail.
Other: to develop spatial awareness and drawing and colouring skills.

DESCRIPTION   The children have a picture of an empty playground to fill in. The teacher describes what is happening in the playground and the children listen and draw what they hear.

PREPARATION   1 Make a copy of Worksheet 1.8 (see back of book) for yourself. Decide on some interesting but easy-to-draw playground activities and draw children doing them (stick figures will do). The activities can be everyday ones (for example, running), or unusual (for example, a dragon coming through the gate!).

2 At the same time, think about how you are going to describe these activities to the class. You may find it useful to write an outline description for yourself.

3 Make a copy of Worksheet 1.8 for each child. If you do not have access to a photocopier, draw a simple playground (just a fence and a corner of a building will do) for the children to copy.

IN CLASS

1 Check the main points of vocabulary with the children, using mime or pictures on the board. Useful words might include: *top, bottom, left-hand, right-hand, corner, middle, girl, boy, by/next to, fence, running, jumping, standing, talking,* and colours.

2 Give out the photocopies of Worksheet 1.8, or draw the empty playground for the children to copy. Explain that you are going to tell them in English where the children are and what they are doing, and that they must draw them.

3 Practise the activity with just one of the children in the picture. Check that the class understand what to do.

4 Tell them that they should just listen the first time you describe the whole picture, not draw. Describe it.

5 Then describe each child in the playground individually, pausing after each one so that the children can start to draw.

As children often take a long time drawing, just give them enough time to start each figure, and then let them finish at the end of the dictation. Explain this if they panic.

6 Describe the picture one more time so that they can check their work, either individually or in pairs.

7 Show them your master picture.

VARIATION

You can adapt this activity to suit the topic you are working on: for example, a house and garden, a birthday party tea, in the street, in a shop, or by the sea.

FOLLOW-UP 1

1 With some pictures, for example of a birthday party tea, you can talk with the children about the picture and ask them what the people in it are saying to each other.

2 The children say these dialogues to each other in pairs, and continue the conversation if possible.

FOLLOW-UP 2

The children can act a 'living picture' like the one they have just drawn, in which each group of children has to say something.

2 Speaking

Teaching children to speak a foreign language can be very rewarding, as they are less self-conscious than older learners. Children love to have little conversations, sing songs, and learn short phrases, and it is easier for them to attain native-like pronunciation. In activities such as 2.2, 'On the farm', or 6.4, 'Happy families', they can repeat key language without it becoming boring.

Children also respond strongly to music and rhythm, and you will find that they are more easily able to learn a chant or a song than a spoken text. Songs and chants are also useful for teaching the stress pattern and rhythm of English—see Chapter 7, 'Songs and chants'.

However, teachers often find speaking a difficult skill to teach, because learners have to master several different elements of language in order to say what they want: vocabulary, pronunciation, structures, functions, and so on. This is why it is easier to teach short, set phrases first, such as everyday classroom language like greetings and requests, or *What's your favourite sport?* in basic information gathering activities such as 2.3, 'A class survey'. This gets the children used to the sound, feel, and rhythm of the language, without having to worry too much about how to formulate what they want to say.

As children get older they become better able to use and manipulate the language, and you can add less tightly controlled activities such as storytelling (for example 2.5, 'The Three Little Pigs'), or information gathering (for example, 2.6, 'A questionnaire on health'). It is important to bear in mind that children need to see the reason for doing the activity—for example, to complete a picture, to find information in order to make a graph, or to put on a performance. This end-product is an important motivating factor, often more important than the topic itself.

A common problem in monolingual classes is that the children lapse into their own language, often through frustration at not having the English to do the task. Choose tasks that are within their capabilities and make it very clear when they can and cannot speak their own language. If the children know that at the end of a task they will be able to have a couple of minutes' 'relaxation' in their own language, they are more likely to keep to the rules and try to do the task in English.

2.1 Simple speaking activities

LEVEL	1, 2, (3)
AGE GROUP	All
TIME	10–20 minutes
DESCRIPTION	Some short, simple activities that develop speaking skills.

Find your partner

AIMS	**Linguistic:** *Hello, what's your name? My name is ….*
PREPARATION	Write the names of well-known people or TV characters on cards. Each name should be written on two cards, and there should be a card for each child.
IN CLASS	1 Give out the cards and tell the children that they are that person and must find their 'twin'. 2 They ask each other questions until they find the child who has the same card.
VARIATIONS	Give the children simple pictures to describe to each other. Alternatively, you can give them halves of pictures and get them to find their other half; or you can give one a picture and the other a written description.

Which one is it?

AIMS	**Linguistic:** Descriptions of people and things: *He/she/it is …, He/she/it has …,* colours, etc.
PREPARATION	Find pictures of people in magazines, cut them out, and mount them on card.
IN CLASS	1 Stick the pictures on the board and get the children to give each one a name. Use them to present and practise describing people. 2 The children work in pairs: one child describes a person and the other has to guess which one.
VARIATIONS	You can use a similar technique with pictures of houses, rooms, towns, or animals.

Hide and seek

AIMS	**Linguistic:** *Is it in …? Yes, it is/No, it's not.*

IN CLASS

1 Give each child an identical picture of a room, or an outdoor scene.

2 The children work in pairs. Each child 'hides' four or five objects in his or her picture (toys, people, coloured mice).

3 They have to ask questions to find out where their partners have hidden their objects. The partner must not lie!

Mime and guess

AIMS

Linguistic: Present continuous and other structures.

PREPARATION

Write or draw several actions such as *eat a banana* or *swim in the sea* on cards or slips of paper.

IN CLASS

1 Give out the cards to individual children or pairs of children.

2 Give the children time to prepare a mime of their action.

3 Get them to do their mime for the rest of the class, who guess the action: for example, *They are eating a banana.*

2.2 On the farm—an information gap activity

LEVEL

1

AGE GROUP

A, B

TIME

20–40 minutes

AIMS

Linguistic: *There is, there are, it's* + colour, *it's in.*
Other: to encourage children to co-operate with each other.

DESCRIPTION

The children work in pairs. Each partner has a copy of the same picture, but with different parts missing. They describe their pictures to each other and draw in the missing parts.

PREPARATION

Photocopy Worksheets 2.2a and b (see end of book), or draw or find a similar picture yourself (you can white out the parts of the picture you don't want), and make copies for the children.

IN CLASS

1 Sketch a few fields with animals in them on the board, like this:

Then ask the children how they could describe them in English. For example: *There are two horses in the big field. They are eating.*

2 Tell the children in their native language that they are going to complete a picture of the farm, and show them the two versions of the picture. Explain that they are going to work in pairs: both partners will have the same picture, but with different parts missing. They are going to take turns to describe the picture and to draw in what is missing.

3 Put the children in pairs and give out the pictures, one of each version to each pair. Make sure there is no peeping! Let them start.

4 When the children have finished, get them to check by looking at each other's pictures.

COMMENTS

1 This kind of activity, where each child has part of the information and can only get the 'whole picture' by asking his or her classmates, is known as an 'information gap' activity. Information gaps are useful as they are easy to prepare, versatile, and create a need to communicate in the children. They can be based on pictures, diagrams, maps, letters, personal fact files, stories, in fact just about anything.

2 If this is the first time you have done an information gap activity, do it with the whole class before the children work in pairs. Divide the class into two halves, A and B. A child from group A describes his or her picture to all the children in group B who then draw, and vice versa.

3 *1000 Pictures for Teachers to Copy* by Andrew Wright has some useful pictures of animals.

2.3 A class survey—favourite sports

LEVEL	2, 3
AGE GROUP	All
TIME	30–60 minutes
AIMS	**Linguistic:** questions with *what*, names of sports. **Other:** gathering and presenting information.
DESCRIPTION	The children ask their classmates what their favourite sports are, then make a bar chart of the result.
MATERIALS	Copies of the questionnaire grid, squared paper for the graphs, coloured pencils.
PREPARATION	Prepare a copy of the questionnaire grid for each child (see In Class, 6).
IN CLASS	1 Ask the children in their native language to call out as many sports as they can think of in two minutes. Write them all on the board.

2 Ask the children if they know the English names of the sports. Write the English names next to the native-language ones.

3 In English, ask one or two children *What's your favourite sport?* and when they have understood the question get the class to repeat it all together. Write the question on the board.

4 They now ask three or four of their neighbours *What's your favourite sport?*

5 Now ask the class, in their native language, if everybody gave the same answer. Ask them if they know which is the most popular sport. Ask them how they could find out.

6 Give out copies of a questionnaire grid like the one below and explain how to fill it in.

Sport	How many?	Total
Football	I I I I	4
Basketball	I I	2

7 The children move around the class, asking each other the questions. Listen in to make sure they are asking in English. If you have a large class, you can divide them into groups of about ten for this stage.

8 When everybody has finished, ask them how they could display the information. You can introduce the idea of a bar chart by stacking up cubes, or drawing squares on the board: one stack per sport, one square or cube per person who likes that sport most.

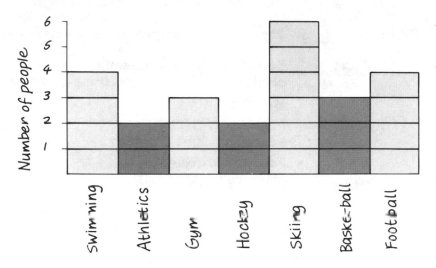

9 Show them how to draw and complete the bar chart.

10 When the bar charts are complete, stick them on a large piece of paper to make a poster.

FOLLOW-UP 1

Use the bar charts to present and practise comparisons.

VARIATION 1

You can use this technique with lots of topics, to suit your children's age and interests—pop music, sports personalities, television programmes, subjects at school—and the language can vary from the very simple questions used here to more complicated ones.

VARIATION 2

Older children who are familiar with angles and percentages can make pie charts to present their survey results.

2.4 Tongue-twisters

LEVEL	**All**
AGE GROUP	**All**
TIME	**15–30 minutes**
AIMS	**Linguistic:** to practise given sounds. **Other:** to play creatively with language.
DESCRIPTION	The children make up tongue-twisters following a given pattern.
PREPARATION	Decide what sounds you want to practise and make up some examples of tongue twisters using these sounds. **Models:** *I saw six silly sausages* (repetition of first consonant) *Fat cats, black bats* (repeated vowel sound)
IN CLASS	**1** Write up some words containing the sounds you want to practise on the board. Include the words you have used in your examples.

sad	black	mad	bad
fat	bat	man	cat

2 Ask the children if they can add any more words to the groups. Older children can look through their books to do this.

3 Write up your tongue twister on the board, and get the children to practise saying it.

4 Ask the children if they can change any of the words. For example: *Bad cats, sad bats.*

5 Put the children in pairs, and let them try to change one or two words in the tongue twister, or make up an entirely new one using yours as a model.

6 When everyone has finished, each pair should say its tongue-twister to the class for everyone to try. You can put up some of the best ones on the wall and start a poster.

FOLLOW-UP	The children can time each other in groups to see how long it takes each child to say their tongue-twister five times (correctly!).

2.5 The Three Little Pigs—a story build

LEVEL 2, 3

AGE GROUP A, B

TIME 25 minutes

AIMS **Linguistic:** to draw on the children's language resources to tell a story.

DESCRIPTION The teacher uses pictures to elicit a story from the children.

PREPARATION 1 Read through the story, adapting it where necessary to suit your children.

2 Practise the board drawings, or make flashcards if you prefer. Board drawings have the advantage of being more flexible, as you can add to them or rub parts out.

IN CLASS 1 Pre-teach any vocabulary you think necessary—for example, *wolf, blow, straw, wood, bricks.* If you tell the story in the past tense, make sure the children recognize the past tenses of verbs such as *blow, build, and run.*

2 Explain to the children that you are going to tell them a story, but that you cannot speak (perhaps you have a very sore throat)! You can only use pictures and mime—they must try and guess what you are trying to say. Give them the title of the story.

3 Put·up or sketch a picture and elicit some sentences from the children. Use gestures such as nodding, shaking your head, or making a puzzled or encouraging face to correct them until you have got more or less what you want. Get one or two children to repeat the sentence.

THE THREE LITTLE PIGS

This is the story of the Three Little Pigs and the Big Bad Wolf.

The first pig built a house of straw.

The second pig built a house of wood.

The third pig built a house of bricks.

One day the Big Bad Wolf was hungry.

He blew down the first pig's house. The little pig ran to his brother's house.

The wolf was still hungry. He blew down the second pig's house. The two pigs ran to their brother's house.

The wolf was still hungry. He went to the third pig's house. He blew and blew and blew, but the house didn't fall down.

He climbed on to the roof and jumped down the chimney.

He fell into the fire! Ooowww! He climbed up the chimney very fast and ran away.

The Three Little Pigs lived happily ever after.

COMMENTS	It is fun not to speak at all, but it can be very frustrating, so be flexible.
VARIATION 1	Stories which include a puzzle work well, especially for older children, but any short story with a strong story line will work. There are some useful pictures and stories in Andrew Wright's book *1000 Pictures for Teachers to Copy* (see Further Reading section).
VARIATION 2	Use Cuisinaire rods to tell the story, fixing them to the board with blu-tak.
FOLLOW-UP 1	The children draw pictures of the story.
FOLLOW-UP 2	The children dramatize the story and perform it for another group.
FOLLOW-UP 3	The children write a modern version of the story, or from the wolf's point of view—see 4.6, 'Story writing'.

2.6 A questionnaire on health

LEVEL	2, 3
AGE GROUP	(A), B, C
TIME	45–60 minutes
AIMS	**Linguistic:** questions and answers: *how often*, frequency vocabulary. **Other:** to develop an awareness of a healthy lifestyle.
DESCRIPTION	The children think about how to keep healthy, and then ask each other questions on health and fitness.
PREPARATION	1 Read through the questionnaire on Worksheet 2.6 (see end of book). Add questions if you wish, and take out any that are not relevant to your children. 2 Make copies of the questionnaire for each child.
IN CLASS	1 In their native language, find out what the children understand by 'healthy'. Ask them if they think they are healthy. Tell them the word in English and ask them what we should do to keep healthy. Note their ideas on the board.

> eat fruit   don't smoke   eat
>   drink milk   do sport   vegetables
> sleep   don't watch too much TV

2 Show them the questionnaire and tell them it is a test of how healthy they are. Explain that they are going to ask each other questions and note down the answers on the worksheet.

3 Using the ideas on the board, practise making questions. For example, if they have suggested 'eat fruit and vegetables', the questions could be *How often do you eat fruit?* and *How often do you eat vegetables?*

4 Put the children into pairs (see 6.1, 'Forming groups'). Give out the questionnaires and get them to practise the questions. You can write the questions on the board for them to refer to.

5 Tell them to put ticks for their own and their partner's answers.

6 Change the pairs and let them start.

7 When they have all finished ask how healthy they are. Who got the most Cs?

<table>
<tr><td>**FOLLOW-UP 1**</td><td>Get the children to write a few 'good health resolutions' in English. This practises using *going to* for plans.</td></tr>
</table>

FOLLOW-UP 1   Get the children to write a few 'good health resolutions' in English. This practises using *going to* for plans.

FOLLOW-UP 2   Get the children to make a 'good health poster'.

FOLLOW-UP 3   Older children can try to make up their own questionnaire on a different topic—you will need to help them with facts and language.

FOLLOW-UP 4   The questionnaire can be given to other groups in school.

2.7 Telling lies

LEVEL   2, 3

AGE GROUP   B, C

TIME   40–50 minutes, or 2 sessions of 20–25 minutes

AIMS   **Linguistic:** asking and answering questions.
Other: memorizing details, to gain confidence.

DESCRIPTION   The children invent an alternative personality for themselves and then are questioned in detail about it by two or three 'Secret Police'. They have to try to escape discovery.

PREPARATION   1 Make copies of the 'Secret file on 003' on Worksheet 2.7, or write an alternative personal history for yourself and make a copy for each pair of children.
2 Make a copy of the blank 'Secret file on 004' for each child (or you can draw one on the board for the children to copy).

IN CLASS   **Part One**
1 Arrange the furniture to look something like this:

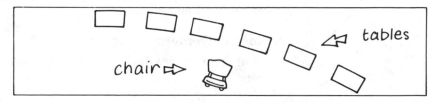

2 Draw a blank 'Secret file' on the board, and check that the children know the questions they need to ask to fill it in.

3 Explain that you are a spy escaping from the Secret Police and that you have invented a new identity for yourself. Show them your 'Secret file on 003'. They are the Secret Police and this is the frontier; if you can answer all their questions correctly you will escape.

4 Ask for four or five volunteers to interrogate you. Explain that the rest of the class are all Secret Police and can hear the answers over a microphone. If you give any wrong answers they can arrest you. Get the volunteers to sit in the questioners' seats. Put the rest of the class in pairs and give out the copies of your 'Secret file on 003'.

5 If you want to, you can add a bit of theatre by arriving at the frontier, showing a guard your passport, he sends you into the office, you say you don't understand anything, etc. Then the interrogators question you.

6 When you have finished, divide the children into groups and get each group to make up a group 'Secret file'. Each member of the group makes a copy of it.

Part Two (You could stop the activity here and take the 'Secret files' in to continue in another lesson.)

7 Regroup the children in such a way that there is one member from each 'Secret file' group in each new group.

8 The new groups set up their frontier posts and take it in turns to be spies and Secret Police. The questioners take the first suspect's 'Secret file' and the questioning starts. The winning team could be the 'Secret file' group that gets most spies across the frontier.

VARIATION

The children have to make up a story to explain where they were between, say, 6 o'clock and 9 o'clock to the police who are questioning them. In the classic version of this activity, 'Alibi', two children make up a story and are questioned separately. The questioners are looking for differences in their answers.

COMMENTS

Be aware of your children's personalities when grouping children: dominant children should not be 'questioners' to sensitive or timid children.

Acknowledgement

I would like to thank Paul Gentle who gave me the idea for this activity.

3 Reading

All children need to learn to read, but when should they start to read in English? There is no hard and fast answer, and each teacher has to evaluate his or her own class. Here are some criteria to bear in mind:

- How well can the children read in their first language?
- Do they need to learn to read in English at this stage?
- Do the children use Latin script in their first language?
- Do the children show an interest in reading in English?
- What are you going to ask the children to read? words? sentences? short stories?

One way into reading with very young children is to read them stories aloud from a picture book. Show them the words and pictures as you read, and they will begin to associate sounds and meaning with written symbols. For ideas on how to use children's books see *The Primary Teacher's Story Telling Handbook* by Gail Ellis and Jean Brewster (see Further Reading).

In this chapter you will find some examples of techniques that you can use with reading texts in your coursebook, and texts of your own. Your coursebook is probably full of texts of one kind or another—dialogues, cartoons, and so on—but you will probably find that they are under-exploited. The most common type of task accompanying a reading text is comprehension questions, but these represent only one of a whole range of techniques that can be used to help, and check, the children's understanding of what they have read. True-false questions are a variation on comprehension questions which children enjoy. Another technique for exploiting texts is given in 3.4, 'Sort it out'.

When choosing reading material for your children, try and find texts that are enjoyable and interesting, so that the children will want to read them. Stories are always popular, and factual texts are an excellent way of linking English with other subjects. Recently, there has been a lot of emphasis on the use of authentic reading material in the language classroom, both for the language content and because children need to learn to interpret non-linguistic cues such as pictures. However, authentic materials for young children (cartoons for example) are often full of idiomatic expressions which make them very difficult to use. Books which suit your children's age and interests may well be too hard linguistically, while books with simple language may be too 'babyish'. There are magazines available that are very authentic looking but written especially for young learners (for instance, *Click* and *Crown*—see Further Reading).

There are many readers for all ages and tastes, and it is an excellent idea to build up a class library and to encourage your children to use it. Some teachers like their children to have a reading card on which they note down the books they have read and their opinion of them. The teacher makes a note of achievements and any problems; this can be a valuable way of measuring progress in reading. For more information on using readers, see *Class Readers* by Jean Greenwood in this series (see Further Reading).

3.1 Making greetings cards—read and draw

LEVEL	(1), 2
AGE GROUP	A, B
TIME	30 minutes
AIMS	**Linguistic:** to develop intensive reading skills. **Other:** to practise drawing, colouring, and cutting-out skills.
DESCRIPTION	The children follow simple written instructions to make a Mother's Day greetings card. The technique can be adapted for other age groups and occasions.
MATERIALS	A large copy of the picture (optional), flashcards (see Preparation, 4), a copy of Worksheet 3.1 (see end of book) for each child, a piece of thin card for each child, an envelope for each card or a large piece of paper, coloured pencils, scissors, and glue.
PREPARATION	1 Make the card yourself so that the children can see a finished one.

2 Make a copy of Worksheet 3.1 for each child.

3 Cut a piece of thin card approximately 50cm x 15cm for each child.

4 Make flashcards with the words *draw*, *colour*, *cut*, *stick*, and the English names of colours on.

IN CLASS

1 If necessary, teach the children the verbs and colours from the worksheet and put flashcards on the wall for reference while they are working. This can be done in the previous class.

2 Talk a little with the children in their native language about mothers (and about carers in general as some children are not cared for by their mothers but by fathers, grandmothers, foster parents, or childminders), what they do for the children and for the family, and go on to talk to them about Mother's Day. Do they have Mother's Day in their country? If so, what do they do for their mothers/carers on that day?

3 Tell them that in Britain children give cards to their mothers/carers on Mother's Day. Show them the card that you have made and tell them they are going to make one for the person that looks after them.

4 Put up or sketch a big copy of the picture on the board and check that the children know the English vocabulary, writing it in like this if you think it is necessary:

5 Check that the children know how to read the colours by holding up flashcards with the English words on them and asking them to hold up a pencil of the corresponding colour.

6 Give each child a piece of card and show them how to fold it in half.

7 Give each child a worksheet. Read through the instructions together, checking at each step that the children understand what they are going to do.

8 Let the children start. Go around the class helping out where necessary. The language problems will mostly be vocabulary ones so you will be able to refer them to the board and flashcards.

9 When they finish let them look at each other's cards. Show them how to write 'To ...' and 'With love from ...' on the inside, telling them to write the name of their carer after 'To' and their own name after 'from'.

10 Finally, give out the envelopes and show the children how to write an address.

VARIATION	Instead of giving the children ready-made envelopes, you can show them how to fold one themselves as a listening task (see 1.6, 'Make an instructions machine', for the technique).

3.2 Problem solving

LEVEL	2, (3)
AGE GROUP	(A), B, C
TIME	30 minutes
AIMS	**Linguistic:** numbers, reading for detail. **Other:** basic arithmetical skills, co-operation between children.
DESCRIPTION	The children read simple arithmetical problems in English and solve them.
PREPARATION	1 Prepare some mathematical problems in English (the children's maths book is a good source). If your children are not familiar with British money, use their own country's money. 2 Make copies of the problems.
IN CLASS	1 Put the children in pairs. Write a problem on the board and ask them to try and solve it. Go over it with the whole class and sort out any difficulties with language or arithmetic. 2 Give out the problems and let the children start. Tell them that they can discuss the problems with their partner in their native language if they like. 3 Wait until everyone has finished and go through the answers with the whole class.
EXAMPLES	

> 1 Michael has got two red bricks and four yellow bricks. He has got ...... bricks.
>
> 2 Ann has got ten sweets. She gives three to her friend Sally. Now she has got ...... sweets.
>
> 3 There are usually twenty children in the class. One day four children are ill and do not come to class. That day there are ...... children in class.
>
> 4 It is Peter's birthday. He has got twelve packets of nuts. He has got six friends. He gives ...... packets to each friend.

> **5** Angela likes toy cars. She goes to a toy shop. The big cars cost one pound, the small cars cost seventy-five pence each. Angela has got five pounds. She buys two big cars and four small cars. Now she has got ...... pence.
>
> (100 pence = 1 pound)

VARIATION

Another way of presenting this activity is to write each problem on a file card: give each child a card, and when he or she finishes it they pass it on to someone else and find one they have not done.

COMMENTS

Talk to the children's maths teacher to find out their level in maths. The examples given here vary from very simple to very difficult.

3.3 The washing line

LEVEL

2, (3)

AGE GROUP

B, C

TIME

20–30 minutes

AIMS

Linguistic: to practise intensive reading.
Other: to develop the skill of making logical deductions.

DESCRIPTION

The children put together information from several sentences to find out which clothes belong to which person, and where they live.

PREPARATION

1 Make enough copies of Worksheet 3.3 (see end of book) so that the children have one between two, or copy the worksheet on to a large poster or the board.

2 Do the worksheet yourself so that you are aware of the logic needed to solve the puzzle and can help the children.

IN CLASS

1 Pre-teach or revise the names of the clothes.

2 Draw a block of flats on the board and check that the children know the names of the floors—ground floor, first floor, and so on. (If you are teaching American English you will have to adapt the worksheet to read first floor, second floor, and so on.)

3 Write the names of the people on the board: Dawn, Peter, Bob, Jane and Mary, Anna. Tell the children that they all live in the flats on different floors.

4 Explain that they all share a washing line in the garden. One day it was very windy and all the clothes on the washing line blew off and landed in a heap on the ground. The children are going to work out who each piece of clothing belongs to, and where the owners live. How? By reading the information and thinking hard!

5 Put the children into pairs. Give out the worksheets and give them a little time to read all the sentences.

6 Then ask them (in English if possible) who the football shirt belongs to, and what floor that person lives on. Ask those who get the answer right to tell the others (in their native language if necessary) how they worked it out.

7 Let the children continue. Go around encouraging and giving hints where necessary, but try and get them to help each other first. If they find it very difficult, draw this grid on the board to help them:

NAME	FLOOR	CLOTHES
Dawn		
Peter		
Bob		
Jane		
Mary		
Anna		

8 When they finish, get them to compare their answers before checking the whole class's answers.

VARIATIONS

This technique can be used with other topics, for example:
– which cars and bicycles belong to which family
– which picnic or shopping basket belongs to which family
– which toys belong to which child
– which school report belongs to which child.

3.4 Sort it out

LEVEL   2, 3

AGE GROUP   B, C

TIME   30 minutes

AIMS

Linguistic: to practise intensive reading, to help children to learn how texts are organized.

DESCRIPTION

Give the children two or three texts that have been mixed together to form one text. The children have to read it and separate out the original texts.

PREPARATION

1 Either use Worksheet 3.4 (see end of book), or choose two or three short texts from your coursebook, or any other source. Mix the sentences together to make one text. It is best not to change the order of the sentences as this would make the activity very difficult. The easiest way to mix up the texts is by retyping them using a word processor.

2 If the original texts do not have a title, think of one for each text.

3 Make a copy of the mixed-up texts for each pair of children.

IN CLASS

1 Write the titles of the texts on the board, mixed up. For example:

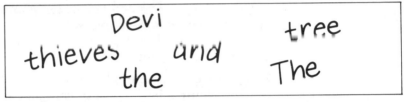

2 Tell the children how many titles there are and ask them to try and sort them out.

3 Tell the children that you are going to give them the texts that go with the titles, but that they are mixed up too, and that the children have to sort them out.

4 Give out the worksheets and let them start. Give them a hint: a good way of doing the sorting is to underline the sentences from each text in a different colour.

5 As they finish, ask them to compare their answers in pairs before going through the texts with the whole class.

6 Feedback
The first few times they do this activity some of the children will find it difficult. It is therefore very useful to give them an opportunity to think about how they have done the task. The more successful children should be encouraged to share their 'tips' with everybody in the class. Their strategies will probably be things like:

– looking for the story-line
– noting names and pronouns
– noting connectors like *and, but,* and *because*
– noting sequencers like *first, then,* and *next*
– noting punctuation.

You can make these strategies explicit by asking the children to look for a 'clue' in each sentence that links it to the next one: these clues could be to do with grammar, vocabulary, or logic. A more explicit way of doing this is to ask them to underline pronouns referring to one person or thing in one colour. Similarly, you can ask them to focus on connectors, punctuation, sequencers, and so on. You will find that if you provide the children with these tools they will enjoy the challenge of sorting out the texts.

VARIATION 1	Instead of mixing up two texts, put three or four nonsense sentences into a text and ask the children to find them.
VARIATION 2	Use one text and mix up the order of the sentences within it.
VARIATION 3	Use one text and vary the details within it: for example, the colour of people's clothes, their names, or how many of a particular item, and ask the children to spot the mistakes.
COMMENTS	1 The activity is easier if you type out each sentence on to a different line, make photocopies for your children, stick them onto card, and cut them into sentence strips. In this way the children can manipulate the text, moving the sentences around as they sort them out.
	2 If you are not able to photocopy, you could copy each of the sentences onto a large piece of card and stick them on to the blackboard or a felt board. The children rearrange the strips.
	3 See also 5.8, 'Colour parsing'.

3.5 At a restaurant

LEVEL	(1), 2, 3
AGE GROUP	B, C
TIME	30 minutes
AIMS	**Linguistic:** to practise scanning, restaurant phrases and vocabulary, and requests. **Other:** basic arithmetical skills.
DESCRIPTION	The children read some dialogues that take place in a restaurant and, using the menu, calculate the customers' bills.
PREPARATION	Make a copy of Worksheet 3.5 (see end of book) for each child.

Alternatively, you can use a suitable dialogue from your textbook, or make one up, and make up a menu to go with the dialogue. If the children are not familiar with British money, you may want to use their own currency.

IN CLASS

1 Pre-teach or revise any vocabulary you feel necessary. Draw a picture of a restaurant scene like the one below on the board and elicit the words *waiter*, *customer*, *menu*, and *bill*.

2 Give out the worksheets and let the children read the instructions. Check that they understand that they have to read the dialogue, write out the bill (looking at the menu for the prices), and find the total.

3 The children start, working either individually or in pairs. Go around encouraging them. If they have a problem get them to help each other first, but you can help them if necessary.

Remember that when the children do activities like these, they need to learn to understand the general gist without worrying that they may not understand every single word.

4 As they finish, ask them to check their answers in pairs before you go through them with the whole class.

FOLLOW-UP

This activity leads nicely into a restaurant role play.

VARIATION 1

Ask the children to work out the individual bills.

VARIATION 2

You can use this technique in any situation where money changes hands—at the supermarket, buying clothes, or at the fair.

3.6 Making milkshakes

LEVEL 2, 3

AGE GROUP B, C

TIME Part One: 20 minutes
Part Two: 45 minutes

AIMS **Linguistic:** to practise scanning, and reading instructions.
Other: basic cookery skills.

DESCRIPTION **Part One:** The children read some shopping lists and match them to the appropriate recipe.
Part Two: They choose a recipe and make it.

MATERIALS Copies of Worksheets 3.6a and b (see end of book) or texts on card, ingredients and utensils for the recipes, aprons, cloths for cleaning up.

PREPARATION 1 Follow the recipes yourself so that you will be able to help the children if necessary.

2 If you are going to make the recipes in class and do not have a school cooking fund, tell the children to bring in the ingredients and utensils.

3 Make copies of the worksheets for the children, or copy them on to the board or big posters.

IN CLASS **Part One**

1 Ask the children what they need to do if they are going to do some cooking—choose a recipe, make a list of the ingredients, go to the shops.

2 Explain that they are going to look at five shopping lists and answer some questions about them. Give out the worksheets and tell the children to read all the questions first, and then look at the lists to find the answers.

As this activity is to encourage the children to read quickly and to find specific information (to scan), it is a good idea to give them a time limit of five minutes.

3 Ask the children to check their answers in pairs before going through them with the whole class.

4 Give the children the three recipes, and tell them to match each recipe with a shopping list (there will be two lists left over). Give them a time limit of five minutes.

5 Ask the children to check their answers in pairs before you go through them with the whole class.

Part Two
You can do this in a second lesson.

6 Now ask the children to decide which recipe they like best, and then to find someone else who likes the same recipe. In this way, you can make pairs or groups according to who wants to make what.

7 Pre-teach or revise the essential vocabulary, perhaps drawing a 'kitchen robot' like this on the board for reference.

Hold up each utensil and ask its English name.

8 Get the children to read through the recipe they have chosen and to make a list of the utensils they will need.

9 Organize the classroom and ask each pair or group to get everything they need ready. Then let them start.

COMMENTS

If these recipes are not suitable for your class, you can use the same techniques with other recipes: triple decker sandwiches or fruit salad are fun to do. There are examples of children's recipe books under 'Creative activities' in the Further Reading section. There are also recipes in the Mary Glasgow magazines *Click* and *Crown*.

3.7 Your lucky number

LEVEL	**2, 3**
AGE GROUP	**B, C**
TIME	**25–30 minutes**
AIMS	**Linguistic:** to practise reading for detail, numbers, arithmetical terms. **Other:** to develop basic arithmetical skills.
DESCRIPTION	The children read and follow a set of instructions, and do arithmetic in order to find out their 'lucky number'.
PREPARATION	Make a copy of Worksheet 3.7 (see end of book) for each child, or copy the instructions on to a poster or the board.
IN CLASS	**1** Ask the children in their native language if they are superstitious: do they have lucky charms, lucky colours, or lucky numbers? Tell them that they are going to find out their lucky number in English. **2** Check any key vocabulary words you think necessary: for example, *add*, *subtract*, *count*, *odd*, *even*. **3** Give out the worksheets. Do the first instruction all together and then let them continue on their own. **4** Go round the class, helping if necessary, but wherever possible get the children to help each other.
COMMENTS	Adapt the instructions to suit your class. You may like to talk to their maths teacher and include the kind of maths they are working on at the moment.
FOLLOW-UP	When everyone has finished, get the children to group themselves according to their 'lucky numbers' and find out two or three things they have in common.

4 Writing

The question of when to start teaching children to write in English is closely linked to that of when to start teaching them to read. Similar criteria apply:

- How well can the children read and write in their own language?
- Do they need to be able to write in English at this stage?
- Do they know the Latin script?
- Do they show an interest in writing?
- Will the English spelling system interfere seriously with what they are learning in their own language?
- Are you going to ask them to copy or to be creative?
- To write words, sentences, or stories?

In general, it is best to introduce English through listening and speaking first, then reading, and writing last. It is important to evaluate the needs and abilities of your own children.

For young children, pictures are very important. Ask them to draw a picture first (for example, 'What I did at the weekend'), and then to write a short caption for it. It is usual to ask them to copy words and short sentences first—to practise their handwriting as much as their English. These short sentences and words should reflect themes connected with the children's schoolwork or daily lives, and be linked with pictures and posters around the room.

But writing is much more than the simple mechanics of getting the words down: it also involves being creative, spelling, grammar, punctuation, choice of appropriate words, sentence linking, and text construction; and, for older children, having ideas about content, and the ability to be self-critical and to edit their own work. The children learn some of these skills when they learn writing in their first language, but others have to be taught explicitly in the English class.

Correction

When you correct writing you are correcting two things: (1) the text itself: are the ideas good? Are they put together in a way which is easy to follow? and (2) is the English correct? A child might invent an excellent story but be unable to get it down in accurate English: it is essential to recognize and praise inventiveness as well as pointing out language mistakes.

Read the child's written work first for its content, if possible with the child at your side, so that you can make comments and talk about the story together. It is important to make children feel that you appreciate their work and are not simply looking for mistakes in their English.

With older children who can write confidently, point out major errors in the English and ask them to write the story again. With very advanced learners, don't correct the language, but ask them to try to think of the correct English.

If you want to display the children's work, you can ask them to write out a neat version.

4.1 Variations on a gap

LEVEL	2, 3
AGE GROUP	B, C
TIME	15–30 minutes
AIMS	**Linguistic:** vocabulary (adjectives, opposites) and word order. **Other:** to stimulate the imagination.
DESCRIPTION	The children fill in gaps in short English texts. The first variations are suitable for younger learners and beginners and then they increase in difficulty and the maturity required.
PREPARATION	1 Prepare texts as explained in each activity. 2 Make copies for the children (at least one between two).
IN CLASS	**Picture gaps**

Choose a suitable text and rewrite it, substituting pictures for some of the words. The children should write the words, perhaps with the help of their picture dictionaries.

EXAMPLE

This is my 🐱 _____. She eats 🐟 _____ and drinks 🍶 _____.

Adjective fill

Choose or write a description which has seven or eight adjectives in it that can easily be changed for others. The children read the description and draw a picture of it. Then they change the adjectives and draw a picture of their new description.

EXAMPLE

> Jenny gets up   (late). She drinks a
>   (cold) cup of tea and eats some toast.
> She goes to school in a   (yellow) bus.

Opposites

Choose or write a text, including seven or eight words which
have 'opposites'. Give the children a copy and ask them to write
the opposites in the spaces by the original words.

EXAMPLE

> An old witch lives in a   (big) house in a
>
> wood. She has a   (short) nose and
>
> (black) hair.

Other words

Choose or write a text about a very neutral person. It should
contain some description and some action. Put the children in
pairs or groups of three and tell them to change the text,
imagining that the person is an animal—for example, a mouse, a
lion, or a hippopotamus. When they have finished, let the
children read each others' texts.

EXAMPLE

> Mrs Williams is a teacher. She is tall and thin and has fair
> hair. Her favourite food is fish and chips.
>
> Mrs Williams is a
> hippopotamus. She is short
> and fat and has grey hair.
> Her favourite food is grass.

No gaps

Choose or write a very basic text that contains no adjectives or
adverbs. Give the children a copy and get them to put in
adjectives and adverbs where they think suitable. This example is
adapted from *Chatterbox 3*, page 52:

EXAMPLE

> The Parthenon is a building in Athens. The Greeks built it
> 2,400 years ago. It is on a hill called the Acropolis.
> The Acropolis was the city of the kings in Athens.
>
> Adjectives: Ancient   big   first   beautiful

4.2 The other day ...

LEVEL	2, 3
AGE GROUP	B, C
TIME	**30 minutes**
AIMS	**Linguistic:** vocabulary, to learn how a story is constructed. **Other:** to use the imagination.
DESCRIPTION	The children write a story one line at a time, folding their papers over and passing them on after each sentence. The final story will be a nonsense story made up of several children's sentences.
PREPARATION	1 Read through the story in Worksheet 4.2 (see end of book) and adapt it for your class, or write a similar story yourself. 2 Make a copy of the story for each child.
IN CLASS	1 Tell the children that they are going to write a story together. 2 Pre-teach or revise the vocabulary needed. 3 Give out the worksheets and show the children how to fold them over so that they can only see the first sentence. Then read the first sentence together and explain that they should write the end of the sentence, and then fold the paper over so that the next child cannot see what they have written, and pass it on. 4 Continue until they have completed all the sentences. Then put the children in groups of four or five and let them read one another's stories and choose the one they like best. Then either they or you can read their favourite stories to the class.
FOLLOW-UP	Ask the children to illustrate their favourite stories and then make a class book of them. (See 8.10, 'Making books'.)
VARIATION	Play 'Consequences' with older children. The stages of the story are: ......[Boy] met (fold the page over) ......[Girl] (fold). He said: ...... (fold). She said: ...... (fold). And the consequence was ....

4.3 The chocolate cake

LEVEL	3
AGE GROUP	C
TIME	45 minutes
AIMS	**Linguistic:** to practise writing spontaneously, listening to stories, reading a dialogue with correct pronunciation, stress, and intonation. **Other:** to stimulate the children's imagination.
DESCRIPTION	The teacher tells the children a story that leads to an argument. When the story reaches a critical point the children continue writing who said what.
MATERIALS	Pencils and paper.
PREPARATION	Practise telling the story, using a colleague as 'the class' if possible. Use one of the story outlines below, or invent an appropriate story for your children.
STORY OUTLINE	

THE CHOCOLATE CAKE

A story about Mark, his friend, his sister Sue, and his mother.

Sue's birthday—mother made a beautiful chocolate cake—put in the fridge for Sue's birthday party.

Mark and his friend came home from playing football—tired, dirty, and very hungry.

Opened fridge—saw cake—took a knife—cut a small slice each—ate it—delicious—another slice and another …

Door opened—mother came in—boys had their mouths full— shut the fridge door.

The mother said …

Mark said …

His friend said …

The mother said …

Just then Sue came home.

Sue said …

The boys said …

The mother said …

Sue said …

IN CLASS

1 Set up the situation and put the children in groups of four. Get them to decide who is going to be Mark, his friend, his mother, and his sister. Adapt the number of characters to suit your class. Make sure they all have pencils and that each 'mother' has a sheet of paper.

2 Tell the story. Remember to spend time describing the personalities of the characters and then to build up the suspense until you get to the point where the mother comes in.

3 At this point say *And the mother said ...*, and in a non-storytelling voice say *Now write what the mother said*. Give the 'mothers' a little time to think and write, and then say in your 'story' voice: *And Mark said ....* Tell them to pass the paper to 'Mark' so that he can write. Carry on until each character has written two or three lines.

4 The groups practise saying their dialogues. Check their pronunciation and encourage them to be as dramatic as possible. Each group performs to the rest of the class.

VARIATION

You can use any story with in-built conflict. The following example encourages imagination and creativity:

STORY OUTLINE

THE DRAGON

A story about two children and a dragon.

Two children had to walk through a dark wood to go to school.

Problem—the wood had a dangerous dragon in it.

The dragon was only frightened of one thing—a whistle.

The children always took a whistle—no problem.

Walking along peacefully—suddenly a terrible noise—the dragon!

'Give me the whistle' —looked in the bag—not there!

The dragon came closer.

The girl said ...

The boy said ...

The dragon said ...

Acknowledgement

I learned this technique from Pete Redpath.

4.4 Simple poems

LEVEL 2, 3

AGE GROUP B, C

TIME 30 minutes

AIMS **Linguistic:** to expand vocabulary, creative use of language, use of adjectives.
Other: to give the children a sense of achievement in the foreign language.

DESCRIPTION The children write very simple poems on a given theme, where each line is made up of an adjective and a noun.

MATERIALS Pencils and paper.

PREPARATION Prepare a short adjective-noun poem yourself or use the one below:

Summer
Hot days
Cold ice cream
Yellow sand
Blue water
Big waves
Small fish.

IN CLASS 1 Write your poem on the board and then read it out loud to the class. Ask them if they can see the pattern of the lines and if they can add any more.

2 Tell them that they are going to write a similar poem, and either give them the topic or get the class to agree on one. The first time you do this activity it is a good idea to choose something that is very familiar, such as 'birthdays', or something tangible, such as 'outside the window'. Later you can use more abstract ideas like 'pollution', 'what makes me happy', or a visual stimulus such as a picture or sculpture.

3 Get the children to call out English words on the theme. Write them on the board and divide them into adjectives and nouns. (Put other words such as verbs to one side.) Show the children how to combine an adjective and a noun as in the example.

4 Tell them to write their own poems using the words on the board. You might like to put on some gentle music to create a quiet, thoughtful atmosphere.

5 Go round the class while the children are writing, encouraging and commenting on their work. When they are satisfied with their poems get them to write them out neatly. You can either display them on the classroom walls or make a class book of poems.

VARIATION 1

If you think this is too difficult for your children, you could give them a poem and get them to change some of the words in it (see 4.1, 'Variations on a gap', and 7.2, 'Poems, rhymes, and chants to say').

VARIATION 2

Instead of the adjective-noun combination, you could use a verb-adverb combination.

VARIATION 3

The children can write a counting poem from one to ten. Each line could be a noun-adjective combination or a complete sentence, for example:

In the garden

One dog sleeping in the sun
Two cats washing their ears
Three children playing in the grass
Four mothers drinking tea
Five trees with green leaves
Six butterflies flying in the sky
Seven clothes on the line
Eight birds in a tree
Nine clouds full of rain
Ten flowers with yellow heads.

4.5 Name poems

LEVEL   2, 3

AGE GROUP   B, C

TIME   30 minutes

AIMS   **Linguistic:** to expand vocabulary, creative use of language.
                   Other: to give the children a sense of achievement in the foreign language.

DESCRIPTION   The children write a very simple poem, based on the first letters of a chosen word, for example their name.

IN CLASS   1 Write the letters of your name on the board like this:

SARAH

Ask the children to think of English words beginning with the letters. Make sure you get a variety of parts of speech—nouns, adjectives, and verbs. Then put a variety of 'little words' in a circle—for example, *a, the, and, with, on, in, at.*

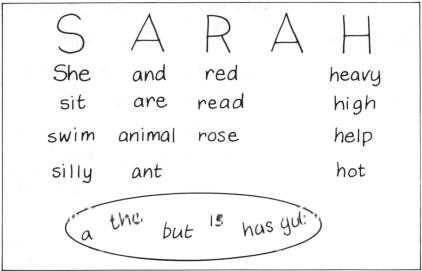

S	A	R		A H
She	and	red		heavy
sit	are	read		high
swim	animal	rose		help
silly	ant			hot

a the but is has you

2 Get the children to help you choose words from the board to make up a short poem where each letter of your name begins a line. You could have just one word per line, or you could have longer lines, for example:

She likes plants		Sitting
Animals		And
Red roses	or	Reading
And		Are her
High places		Hobbies

3 Now ask the children to do the same with their own names. The poems can be displayed on the walls.

Acknowledgement
I would like to thank Paula Vázquez for giving me the ideas for 4.4 and 4.5.

4.6 Story writing

LEVEL	2, 3
AGE GROUP	B, C
TIME	30 minutes +
AIMS	**Linguistic:** to write a short, cohesive text. **Other:** to encourage creative writing and imagination.
DESCRIPTION	The children write simple stories.
MATERIALS	Pencils and paper, pictures, blu-tack (see individual activities).
PREPARATION	See individual activities.

IN CLASS

Following an example

1 Read or tell the children a simple story in English, for example *Where's Spot?* by Eric Hill or one of the story ideas in this book—see 1.2, 'The Frog family', 2.5, 'The Three Little Pigs', or 1.5, 'The Pied Piper'.

2 Ask the children to write a similar story, illustrate it, and perhaps make a book. (See 8.10, 'Making books'.)

Stories on a theme

1 Choose a general theme—for example, 'Summer holidays', 'Parties', or 'Witches', and write it in the middle of the board.

2 Ask the children to draw pictures connected to the title and stick them up on the board.

3 When you have a boardful, put the children in groups of three or four and tell them to invent a story, using three or four of the pictures on the board.

Beginning, middle, and end

1 Draw three shapes like these on the board:

2 Tell the children that they are the beginning, the middle, and the end of a story. Ask them either to suggest words for each box, or to stick or draw a picture in each box.

3 Put the children in groups of three or four and get them to write a story using some words from each box.

Modern fairy stories

1 Tell the children a fairy story like 'Little Red Riding Hood' or 'The Three Little Pigs' (see 2.5).

2 The children write a modern version.

Stories from pictures and words

1 Find some pictures that make a story.

2 Put the pictures on the board one by one and ask the children for ideas and English words that go with each picture.

3 Then put the children in groups of three or four to write the story.

Writing speech bubbles

1 Find or draw a series of pictures showing two or more people.

2 Stick empty speech bubbles coming out of their mouths. Photocopy one for each pair of children.

3 The children write what they think the people are saying in the bubbles.

If you do not have access to a photocopier, give each speech bubble a number and stick the pictures around the classroom walls. The children write the numbers in their exercise books and write what the people are saying by each number. When they have finished writing, they can compare their ideas and perhaps write the best ones on the pictures.

Stories from pictures

1 Cut pictures out of magazines and give four or five to each group of three or four children.

2 Each group makes up a story which includes all their pictures.

COMMENTS

Story writing is the most relevant kind of writing for children. These ideas help to get children started on writing stories, although they do not provide an exhaustive guide to the process of teaching creative writing. See the introduction to this chapter for some tips, and the Further Reading section for more detailed advice.

5 Vocabulary and grammar

Young children are quick to learn words, slower to learn structures. This may be because words have tangible, immediate meanings whereas structures are less obviously useful—after all 'Pencil!' often obtains the same result as 'Can I have a pencil?' They also seem to learn phrases holistically: for example, 'I've got' is learned as a single item 'Ivegot' (/aɪvɡɒt/), rather than analysed into its separate parts. So in order to teach structures to young children, we need to repeat the same structures over and over again in different meaningful contexts, using a variety of vocabulary. In some of the newer coursebooks, this recycling of structures is built in; if it isn't, teachers need to add it themselves, either by going back to previous chapters or by including extra material in their lessons.

Older children are more able to analyse the language they hear and see, and separate it into its component parts. They can make new expressions from elements of ones they have already learned. You may find that they mix their own language with English to make hybrid sentences to express their meaning: for example, 'My cat is *gris*' (grey). The explicit teaching of grammar goes in and out of fashion; certainly teaching grammar for its own sake can be very dry and does not necessarily lead to being able to use the language effectively. On the other hand, an understanding of the structure of a language within meaningful contexts is a powerful tool for children to have, a tool with which they can create meaning.

Vocabulary is best learned when the meaning of the word(s) is illustrated, for example by a picture, an action, or a real object. The children should then meet and use the word(s) in relevant contexts, in order to 'fix' them in their minds. This helps establish their relationship to other words, so that a vocabulary network is built up (see 5.2).

Both vocabulary and grammar need to be taught in context and the children should always to be given plenty of opportunities to use the language that they have learned in class. This means that they do not just learn the rules superficially, but put them into practice in order to communicate.

5.1 Flashcard ideas

LEVEL

All

AGE GROUP

All

TIME

10 minutes+

AIMS

Linguistic: to present and revise vocabulary, to drill structures and functions, to help children relate words to images.

DESCRIPTION

Flashcards (picture cards) are an invaluable way of introducing and revising vocabulary, and can also be used to drill simple structures and functions.

PREPARATION

1 Get your children, colleagues, friends, and acquaintances to bring you colour magazines of all types—women's magazines, children's comics, travel magazines, nature magazines, etc.

2 Go through them from time to time and cut out any pictures that you think could be useful, for instance to illustrate topics, nouns, verbs, adjectives, structures, situations, or functions.

3 Put the pictures into categories.

4 When you are going to use the pictures stick them on thin card and, if you are going to use them a lot, cover them with sticky-backed plastic or a thin plastic bag.

IN CLASS

1 Show the children a flashcard with a picture on it. Say the English word clearly, then they repeat it all together. Go on to the next card.

2 When you have shown them about ten cards (the number depends on the age of the children and the difficulty of the words) go back to the beginning and hold up the first card again.

3 This time wait and see if anyone can remember the word. There is usually at least one child who can more or less say the word; give this child encouragement and help with pronunciation, then use him or her as a model for the rest of the class. Continue with the rest of the cards. This technique encourages the children to listen to you carefully and stops them from being simply passive absorbers (or non-absorbers!).

FOLLOW-UP 1

Prepare a set of word cards to go with the set of pictures you want to work on. Stick the word cards on the board, give out the pictures, and ask the children to stick them on the board beside the word they go with.

FOLLOW-UP 2

Give each child a flashcard which illustrates something easy to mime. They should not let anyone else see it. Ask the children in turn to mime what is on their card to the class. The rest of the class has to guess the English word.

FOLLOW-UP 3

Prepare a set of cards with two pictures of each object. Give out the cards to the class and ask each child to find another with the same object by asking questions such as *Have you got a (cat)?*

FOLLOW-UP 4

Use the cards as cues for structures or functions. For example, a swimming pool could be the cue for *She's swimming, She can swim,* or *Let's go swimming.*

Pairs of cards can be used to practise comparatives, for example: *This car is bigger than that car,* or to find something that both cards have in common, for example: *They are both red,* or a difference: *This car has four doors and that car has two doors.*

COMMENTS

1 You could also draw your own flashcards, or, if you don't feel very confident about your drawing ability, copy pictures from books. An invaluable book is *1000 Pictures for Teachers to Copy* by Andrew Wright (see the Further Reading section).

2 For more ideas on how to use flashcards, I strongly recommend *Pictures for Language Learning* by Andrew Wright (see Further Reading).

5.2 Vocabulary networks

LEVEL

2, 3

AGE GROUP

B, C

TIME

20–30 minutes

AIMS

Linguistic: to present and practise groups of related words.
Other: to practise using dictionaries.

DESCRIPTION

An idea for presenting groups of words.

MATERIALS

Bilingual or picture dictionaries.

PREPARATION

Copy the diagram (see below).

IN CLASS

1 Give out copies of the following diagram. If you do not have access to a photocopier, draw it on the board and get each child to copy it on to paper.

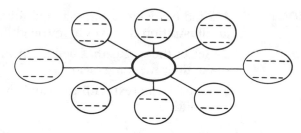

2 Write the topic in the middle circle in English, and then ask each child to put a word in their own language (related to the topic) on the bottom line of each of the outer circles.

3 Then, either in groups, or letting the children ask freely around the class, get them to try and fill in the English translations on the top lines of the outer circles. As they run out of ideas let them turn to dictionaries, and if all else fails allow them to ask you.

4 Finally, ask them to draw a picture of the word in each circle.

COMMENTS

1 It is generally accepted that vocabulary is best learned (and taught) in groups of related words. Such groups are sometimes referred to as 'lexical sets' or 'word families'. For more ideas see the Further Reading section at the end of the book.

2 As always with translation and dictionaries, you need to be careful that the translation is appropriate.

Acknowledgement
I would like to thank Martin Melia for this idea.

FOLLOW-UP

The children can make a poster of the word family they have worked on.

5.3 Guess the words

LEVEL

2, 3

AGE GROUP

B, C

TIME

25 minutes

AIMS

Linguistic: to present vocabulary, to practise guessing meaning from context.

DESCRIPTION

The children read a text that is mostly in their first language but has some English words mixed into it. They use the context to guess the meanings of the English words.

PREPARATION

1 Find or invent a suitable text for your children, if possible with an illustration that will help the children's comprehension.

2 Select the words that will be in English (the context should make their meaning clear).

3 Rewrite the text with the English words and make copies for the children.

IN CLASS

1 Write the title of the text on the board and get the children to look at the picture. Ask them what they think the text is about and to suggest some words, both in English and their first language, that they think will be in the text.

2 Tell them the text is in their own language but that you have hidden some English words in it. Give out the copies and ask them if they can tell you the English words.

3 They read the text again, and in pairs try and work out what the English words mean. You can make this easier by giving them all the translations in a box and asking them to pick out the most suitable one.

FOLLOW-UP

This activity only introduces the words—now the children should be given a chance to use them in context.

5.4 A very long sentence

LEVEL

1, 2

AGE GROUP

B

TIME

15 minutes

AIMS

Linguistic: to activate vocabulary.
Other: to exercise the children's memory, to have fun.

DESCRIPTION

Going round the class, the children repeat the base sentence and add one word to it.

PREPARATION

Think of a base sentence appropriate to the topic you are working on at the moment, for example:

Food: *I went to market and bought ...*
Toys: *For my birthday I got ...*
Animals: *I went for a walk and I saw ...*
Body: *I saw a monster with ...*

IN CLASS

1 Say the base sentence and make sure the children understand it. Drill it a couple of times to help them remember it, for instance by using the 'invisible reading' technique (see 7.1, 'Action songs': 'Bingo') or doing a back chain drill like this:

bought
and bought
market and bought
went to market and bought
I went to market and bought

2 Ask the children to suggest ways of finishing the sentence. For example:

I went to market and bought one apple.
I went to market and bought one apple and two fish.

3 When they have got the idea of making a very long sentence, start the game. Get the children to sit in circles of eight to ten (the game does not work well if the groups are larger). Each child says the sentence and adds one more item. You can make the activity co-operative by asking the other children to help if someone can't remember all the items, or competitive by giving each child three chances and then eliminating them from the game.

COMMENTS

1 If you have a large class and don't want to split it, arrange the children into teams of three or four who work together to remember the sentence, with a 'spokesperson' who says it to the rest of the class:

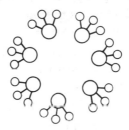

2 This is a good technique for getting less confident children to speak.

5.5 Odd words out

LEVEL   All

AGE GROUP   All

TIME   15–20 minutes

AIMS	**Linguistic:** word families.
	Other: to practise using criteria to define items.
DESCRIPTION	The children are given sets of words and have to decide which of the words does not fit in the set.
PREPARATION	1 Make about ten sets of four or five words, with one 'odd word out' in each set. The words may be 'odd' for a number of reasons, for example:

thematic: *cat, fish, flower, dog*
sound: *cat, dog, hat, fat*
grammatical: *jump, think, swim, fast*
shape/size: *mouse, ant, frog, elephant.*

At first the 'odd' word should be obvious, but as the children get used to doing this kind of task you can make the 'odd' word more subtle. You will often find that the children come up with perfectly reasonable suggestions that you have not thought of. For example, in

strawberry, apple, cabbage, banana

you could say the odd one was the cabbage because it is a vegetable, or the banana because it is not round, or the strawberry because it is small! All are quite acceptable, as long as the children can justify their answer.

2 Write out the sets of words and photocopy them, or write them on the board, or make a poster of them.

IN CLASS	1 Write a set of words on the board and ask the children to tell you which is the odd one out. Make sure they explain their reasoning to you—either in English or in their first language.

2 When they have understood the concept, give them the rest of the sets of words.

3 They can either work individually or in pairs—working in pairs can result in a useful exchange of ideas.

4 As they finish, get them to compare their answers with another child or pair, and then go through the answers with the whole class, asking the children why they chose particular answers.

FOLLOW-UP	When the children are used to doing this kind of exercise, they can have a go at inventing some sets themselves, using their notes and picture dictionaries.
COMMENTS	1 This is a very simple activity, but it requires the children to use the concepts of categories and criteria.

2 It is useful to make a series of sets of words and keep them in a folder in class to give to children who finish another activity early.

5.6 The lost pet

LEVEL 1

AGE GROUP A, B

TIME 20 minutes

AIMS **Linguistic:** to present a structure in context.
Other: to involve the children in a situation or story.

DESCRIPTION The teacher presents a structure using interactive story telling. In this example, the structure is *Is it* + preposition, and is suitable for beginners, but you can adapt the technique to other structures and levels (for example, *Can you/I can, Would you like* ...).

MATERIALS A toy animal or puppet (see 8.7, 'Making puppets').

PREPARATION Hide the toy or puppet in the classroom.

IN CLASS 1 Introduce the situation by drawing or displaying a picture of an empty cage. Tell the children that they are going to imagine that their class has a pet. Tell them what kind of animal it is and ask them to think of a name for it.

2 Tell them that unfortunately, the pet has escaped and that they must find it—in English.

3 Point to the chair and ask them: *Is it under the chair?*

Practise the question and then answer (shaking your head) *No, it isn't.*

4 Ask the class to suggest more questions, using different prepositions and furniture, for example: *Is it in the cupboard?* Look in each place mentioned. Continue until they find the 'pet'.

5 Ask the questions again, this time just pointing to the different pieces of furniture, and encouraging the children to join in as much as possible.

COMMENTS The *Contact English* series by Colin Granger and Tony Hicks has some excellent suggestions for stories—see Further Reading.

VARIATION Another way to introduce this activity is to read *Where's Spot?* by Eric Hill (see Further Reading). See also *The Storytelling Handbook for Primary Teachers* by Gail Ellis and Jean Brewster.

5.7 Keeping the rules

LEVEL	(2), 3
AGE GROUP	(B), C
TIME	20 minutes
AIMS	**Linguistic:** the language of permission, deducing meaning and language rules from context. **Other:** to think about behaviour in public places.
DESCRIPTION	The children match sentences to places and then focus on the language.
PREPARATION	1 Adapt the 'rules' to suit your children's environment (see below). 2 Make copies of the 'rules' (one for every pair of children), or copy them on to a poster or the board.
IN CLASS	1 Ask the children to think of places that have rules and make a list on the board of the places they suggest. Add any others that are in your examples. (The answers to the 'rules' below are: library, swimming pool, football match, park.) 2 Give out the copies of the 'rules', or put up your poster and tell the children that each set of sentences refers to one of the places on the board. Tell them to read the sentences and decide which place they refer to. 3 Let them work in pairs to solve the puzzle and then check the answers. 4 Now ask them to look at the sentences again and find sentences that express obligation to do something (*must*), and then go on to prohibition (*mustn't* or *can't*), permission (*can* or *may*), and impossibility (*can't*). 5 Ask them to write some sentences for another situation—for example, rules for the classroom, in the home, in the kitchen, or how to keep healthy.
FOLLOW-UP	(For advanced classes.) Ask the children to look at the sentences carefully and then to work out a rule about *must*, *mustn't*, *can*, and *can't* (they are followed by an infinitive without 'to'). You will probably have to do this step in the children's first language as the concepts are difficult to express in simple English.

RULES	PLACES
You must keep quiet. You may read any book. You mustn't eat.	_____
You mustn't run. You mustn't wear clothes. You can't drink the water.	_____
You can shout. You must buy a ticket. You mustn't fight.	_____
You can play games. You mustn't walk on the flowers.	_____

Photocopiable © Oxford University Press

COMMENTS

In this activity, the function is that of permission and obligation and is suitable for older children, but you can adapt the technique to other functions and other levels (though it is not suitable for very young children who have not yet developed the ability to deduce grammatical rules from examples of language).

5.8 Colour parsing

LEVEL

2, 3

AGE GROUP

B, C

TIME

30 minutes

AIMS

Linguistic: To learn how a sentence is constructed.

MATERIALS

Coloured chalk, coloured pencils.

PREPARATION

1 Decide which structure you are going to focus on (in this example questions with *like*).

2 Decide on the colours you are going to use. In this case you only need four:

red	*like, love, hate* (verbs)
blue	*I, you, he, she, etc.* (subject pronouns)
yellow	*do, does* (auxiliary verbs)
green	*pizza, coffee, tea, bananas, tomatoes* (nouns)

1 Divide your board into two halves. On the left write some words that fit into the sentence structure you have chosen, like this:

```
like  do   you   she
love     hate   does   he
      coffee  bananas
```

2 Underline a verb in red and invite the children to find and underline other 'red' words. Do the same with the blue, yellow, and green words.

```
like  do   you    she
love     hate   does   he
      coffee  bananas
```

3 Write your model sentence on the right of the board and ask the children to underline the words in the appropriate colours.

```
like  do   you  she    |  Do you like bananas?
love    hate  does  he  |
      coffee   bananas  |
```

4 Show the children how to make other sentences like yours, using the words on the left. Then they make some of their own, either individually or in groups.

5 Ask the children to tell you their sentences and write them under the model.

Ask the children to select sentences that would be suitable for a questionnaire about favourite foods.

```
                    |  Do you like bananas?
                    |  Does he like pizza?
                    |  Do you hate bananas?
```

Do the questionnaire (for the technique, see 2.6, 'A questionnaire on health').

If you are going to use this technique regularly in class, it is worth devising a more complete colour scheme so that you are consistent. Make a poster of it for the classroom wall. Remember that the technique has its limitations and is best used with simple structures—if you are not careful the colour coding becomes more complicated than the structure itself!

6 Games

Games in the language classroom help children to see learning English as enjoyable and rewarding. Playing games in the classroom develops the ability to co-operate, to compete without being aggressive, and to be a 'good loser'.

The games in this chapter are mainly team games, and 6.1, 'Forming groups', gives a number of ways of forming teams. If you make different teams each time you play, the children will get used to working with all their classmates.

Scoring is also an important part of games and 6.2 shows a number of different ways to do this. The rest of the chapter is divided into two parts: games to play in the classroom, and games to play in the gym or outside. Most of the games can easily be adapted to suit the level of your class.

Some of the games involve quite a lot of preparation, but once you have made the materials, you can use them again and again.

6.1 Forming groups

LEVEL	**All**
AGE GROUP	**All**
TIME	**5–10 minutes**
AIMS	To form teams in preparation for playing a game.
DESCRIPTION	Many games are team games. Here are some ways to form pairs, groups, and teams.
IN CLASS	**Using ribbons**

1 The teacher holds a bunch of ribbons like this:

2 The children each take an end.
3 The teacher lets the ribbons go.
4 The children holding the same ribbon form a pair.

Numbering

1 To form pairs: give each child a number, until half the children have one, and then start again from 1.

2 When all the children have a number, those with the same number get into pairs. If you want to make groups of three or more, simply make sure you repeat each number the appropriate number of times.

3 Instead of numbers you can use letters, shapes, colours, foods, etc.

Using a rhyme

1 In this traditional English rhyme the children stand in a circle and each hold out a fist. The 'teller' stands in the middle.

2 The children all chant the rhyme. The 'teller' goes around the circle touching the children's fists in time to the beat. The child who is touched on the word 'more' is the chosen one.

If you want to form pairs ask the children to make two circles with a teller in the centre of each. The children all chant the rhyme together, and the two children chosen form a pair. Continue until all the class are in pairs. If you want groups of three or four you can make three or four circles.

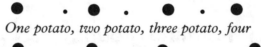

One potato, two potato, three potato, four

● . ● . ● . ●

Five potato, six potato, seven potato, MORE!

Another rhyme you can use is:

. ● ● ●

Red is for roses, roses, roses

. ●

Red is for roses

. ● ●

So out you GO!

Pairs of cards

1 Make two sets of cards with words on. The two sets must be the same and there must be enough cards for all the class. The topic can be vocabulary or grammar you are working on.

2 Divide the class into halves, then give one set of cards to each group.

3 The children take it in turns to mime their cards. When a child recognizes someone miming their card they go and form a pair with him or her.

If you want to form groups of three or four, make three or four sets of the same card.

Using height or age

Ask the children to line up in order of height or age, then divide the line into the number of groups you need.

Making random groups to music

1 Put on some music with a strong beat, and let all the children bounce around to it.

2 Turn down the volume and call out 'Groups of three!' The children get into threes as quickly as they can.

If you want groups of four, call out 'Groups of four!', and so on.

Names in a box

Put all the names of the children in a box, and pull them out two by two, or three by three, depending on how big you want the groups to be. These children form a group.

Acknowledgement

'Using ribbons' and 'Making random groups to music' are adapted from *Drama Techniques in Language Teaching*, by Alan Maley and Alan Duff.

6.2 Scoring games

LEVEL	**All**
AGE GROUP	**All**
TIME	**5–10 minutes**
DESCRIPTION	These are not whole games, but motivating ways of scoring games and quizzes.
IN CLASS	**Football**

You will need to make a large picture of a football on card (see Worksheet 6.2 at the end of the book).

1 Draw a football pitch (or basketball court, or whatever sport most interests your class) on the board like this:

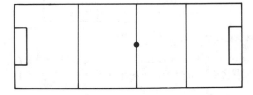

2 Divide the class into two teams, and ask them to decide what their names are, where their home goals are, and which way each team is going.

3 Start the game or quiz.

4 The ball starts at the centre point. When a team wins a point, the ball moves one line towards the other team's goal. If the other team wins a point, the ball moves one line towards their goal.

5 When the ball reaches the goal, that team scores, and the ball goes back to the centre line.

Drawing points

Add a line to a drawing for each point gained. Any simple drawing will do, for example:

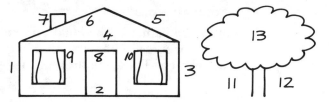

This is a less 'violent' version of the traditional 'Hangman' (see 6.3, 'Word games').

Stepping stones

Draw a simple river on the board with some stones across it, and cut out a cardboard 'frog' for each team.

For each point the frog goes forward one stone. The first team to reach the other side wins.

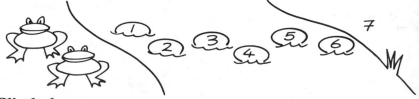

Climb the tower

Draw a ladder going up a tower on the board. For each point the team goes up a rung. The first team to get to the top wins.

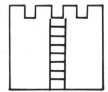

The winners

Each team tries to finish writing a word first—for example THE WINNERS—adding a letter for each point.

Acknowledgement

I learned 'Football' at El Centro Británico, Santiago de Compostela.

Games inside the classroom

6.3 Word games

LEVEL	**All**
AGE GROUP	**All**
TIME	**10–20 minutes**
AIMS	**Linguistic:** vocabulary and spelling.
DESCRIPTION	Word games are very popular with children and there are hundreds of them. Here are some favourite ones.
IN CLASS	**Hangman**

1 One child (the 'thinker') thinks of a word and writes dashes on the board to represent each of its letters.

2 The rest of the children try to guess the letters.

3 If they guess a letter in the word, the 'thinker' writes it over the dash, or dashes, that represent it.

4 For each wrong guess the 'thinker' draws one line of a simple picture of a person hanging from a gallows (see below).

5 If someone thinks they know the word they can guess it, but if they are wrong, another line is added to the figure.

6 The person who guesses the word correctly is the winner. They think of the next word.

7 If nobody guesses the word before the picture is finished, the 'thinker' can think of another word.

EXAMPLE

Vocabulary squares

The children have to find words hidden among other letters.

1 Make a grid and write words in it. The words can be written horizontally, vertically, diagonally, and, for older children, from right to left or bottom to top as well. The words should all be on the same theme. It is a good idea to put all the words in first, make a copy of this, and then fill in the other letters—this way you have a record of where the words are!

2 You can make this game more or less difficult according to the clues you give the children. With younger children, give them the words to look for. With older children, you can tell them the topic, or give them a picture or a written definition of each word.

TRANSPORT

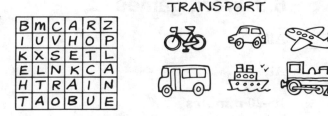

Word chains

Write a 'starter' word on the board. In teams, the children take turns to add a word to either end, as follows:

Words from words

1 Write a long word (or a short sentence) on the board.

2 The children see how many words they can make, using only the letters in the word or sentence.

grandmother ⟹ and, *red,* hot, her,

Tennis

This game is played in pairs and is scored like a game of tennis, but the 'ball' is words.

1 Child A 'serves' a word to child B who 'returns' a word in the same word family.

2 Child A then 'returns' another word, and so on until someone 'misses', that is, cannot think of a word. For example:

Child A: *rabbit*   Child B: *cat*
Child A: *dog*   Child B: *mouse*
Child A: (can't think of a word)
SCORE: love—15

Child A: *table*   Child B: *chair*
Child A: *desk*   Child B: (can't think of a word)
SCORE: 15 all

VARIATION	Instead of word families you could use words beginning with the same letter, or a word beginning with the last letter of the previous word.

Sets of words

1 Prepare a worksheet with words from five or six word families, all mixed up.

2 The children have to sort them out.

EXAMPLE	brother train sister car thin butcher fat tall mother bicycle bookshop supermarket bus

Information gap crosswords

Simple crosswords are easy to prepare and are an excellent way of revising vocabulary or structures.

Information gap crosswords need a little more preparation but are fun, as well as communicative.

1 Prepare the crossword, with the answers.

2 Then draw the blank version twice, putting half the words in one and half the words in the other.

EXAMPLE	 

3 The children work in pairs, each with one version of the crossword. One child defines a word on his or her version, using language, mime, or pictures. The other child has to guess the word and write it on their version.

4 Continue until both children have completed their crosswords.

6.4 Happy families

LEVEL	1, 2, (3)
AGE GROUP	A, B, (C)
TIME	**30 minutes to make the cards, 20 minutes to play**

AIMS	**Linguistic:** questions (*Have you got ...?*), vocabulary: families, colours. **Other:** to take turns in a game.
DESCRIPTION	The children make sets of cards that have something in common; traditionally the sets are a family of mother, father, sister, and brother, but many other sets can be used. The cards are used to play a game where each player collects a set of cards.
MATERIALS	A copy of Worksheets 6.4a and b (see end of book) for each group of four children, thin card, glue, coloured pencils or pens.
PREPARATION	Using Worksheets 6.4a and b, prepare four sets of cards. Colour each set a different colour.
IN CLASS	**1** Show the children your cards jumbled up, and ask for a couple of volunteers to put them into four sets. They should put all the cards of the same colour together to make a family (not, for example, all the sisters together).

2 Divide the children into groups of four. Give each group a copy of Worksheets 6.4a and b, and some thin card. They stick the pictures onto the card, cut out the rectangles, and colour them.

3 When all the cards are finished, demonstrate the game. The aim is to collect one whole family.

a The cards are shuffled and each child is dealt four.

b Players collect cards by asking any other player: *Have you got (Sister Green)?*, and so on.

c If the answer is 'Yes', the other player has to give up their card, and the first child can ask again. If the answer is 'No', it is the next player's turn. The first player to complete a set is the winner.

4 Practise the question and replies if necessary.

5 The children go back to their groups of four and play with their own cards.

VARIATION 1	Instead of families, select another theme which has identifiable sets, for example: **Toys** of different colours and/or sizes **Food:** sets of sweet food, savoury food, drinks, fruit and vegetables **Animals** which live in the sea, in the jungle, in houses, and on the farm.
VARIATION 2	The questions will vary according to the children's level, for example: *Have you got a red bicycle?*

Have you got something from the kitchen?
Have you got an animal which lives in the sea?

Have you got ... could be replaced by other request forms, for example, *Can I have* ..., *I'd like* ..., *or I need* .... Remember to teach the appropriate answers, for example *Here you are.*

6.5 A board game

LEVEL	**All**
AGE	**All**
TIME	**20 minutes' preparation and 20 minutes to play**
AIMS	**Linguistic:** to revise grammar (you can choose which aspects by changing the questions). **Other:** general knowledge, to take turns and win and lose fairly.
DESCRIPTION	The children play a language-based game using a board and dice.
MATERIALS	Stiff card for the boards, thin card for the questions, dice or spinners, counters or coins.
PREPARATION	1 Make a board about 30cm x 30cm, with about 64 squares on it, for each group of children.

It could be the traditional 8 x 8 square board, or you could make a spiral, a path leading to a castle, a race track, etc. The board should also have some squares that allow players to move forward 'free' or that send them back—traditionally these are snakes and ladders.

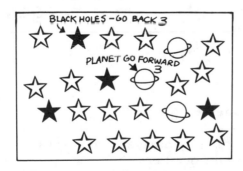 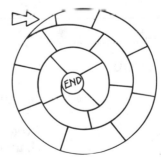

The easiest way to make the boards is to draw a master, then photocopy it and stick it onto stiff card. You can colour it, or ask your children to, and it will last much longer if you cover it with plastic.

2 Then cut some more little squares of card, about the same size as those on your board—these are for the language questions and answers. This way you can use different questions with the same board.

3 Write a question on one side of each small square, and the answer on the other side. Questions may be based on grammar, vocabulary, or general knowledge. You need to make enough questions to cover at least half the board.

You can keep the question cards and board and use them again and again.

IN CLASS

The game is played like this:

1 The players lay out the question cards on the board, question side up. No cards should be put on the 'snakes and ladders' squares.

2 Each player has a counter and each board has a dice or spinner (see 8.5, 'Spinners').

3 The first player throws the dice or spinner and moves their counter. If they land on a square with a question on it, they try to answer it, checking the answer on the back of the square. If they get it right, they move forward the same number of squares again: if they get it wrong, they go back to their previous position. Then it is the next player's turn.

4 The winner is the player who reaches the last square first.

Acknowledgement
The game described here is an adaptation of 'Snakes and ladders' from *Grammar Games* by Mario Rinvolucri (see Further Reading section).

6.6 Carolyn's grammar game

LEVEL

2, 3

AGE GROUP

B, C

TIME

20 minutes +

AIMS

Linguistic: to revise grammar (you can choose which aspects by changing the questions).
Other: to take turns and win and lose fairly.

DESCRIPTION

The children are divided into teams. Each team chooses one question from each category and tries to answer it; the team with the most correct answers wins.

MATERIALS Questions for each category on pieces of card, blu-tak.

PREPARATION 1 Choose categories for the questions. These can relate to what you have been working on in class. For example:

- structures (past forms of verbs, making questions, etc.)
- functions (inviting, apologizing, etc.)
- spelling
- vocabulary
- pronunciation
- general knowledge.

2 Write three or four questions for each category on pieces of card about 10 cm by 15 cm. The number of questions depends on the number of groups that are going to play—it is best to have one more question in each category than there are groups.

IN CLASS 1 Draw the following table on the blackboard, using your own categories. Stick the pieces of card in their places, face down.

2 Divide the class into teams and decide who is going to start.

3 The first team picks a category and a number.

4 The teacher reads out or shows them the card, and they try to answer the question. They get a point for a correct answer. If they give an incorrect answer the teacher asks the next team.

5 The game continues until you have asked each team one question in each category. The winners are the ones with the most points.

COMMENTS 1 Older children could write the questions themselves: this is a good opportunity for them to do some revision. It also adds an extra incentive when they choose their questions, as they may get their own.

2 At first sight this seems to be a very simple, and not very inspiring game. However, the element of chance in it appeals to children and they love it. Try it!

Acknowledgement
Carolyn Gentle taught me this game.

Games outside the classroom

6.7 A treasure hunt

LEVEL	2, 3
AGE GROUP	B, C
TIME	45–60 minutes
AIMS	**Linguistic:** commands, prepositions, *wh-* questions. **Other:** to develop logical thought, to build a team spirit.
DESCRIPTION	The children follow a series of written (or tape-recorded) clues which lead them to a hidden treasure.
MATERIALS	Pieces of paper or card for clues, small prizes for 'treasure'. Cassette players and cassettes, if you record the clues.
PREPARATION	1 Decide on the route of the treasure hunt. You need between 10 and 12 places to hide the clues and somewhere for the treasure itself.

2 Write clues. These should direct the children to the next clue, but not in an immediately obvious way. You can use the clues to reinforce a particular structure such as *wh-* questions, prepositions, or commands. For example:

Where do we eat our lunch?
Look under the piano.

3 Devise a way of checking that the children have actually followed all the clues and not taken short cuts. One idea is to prepare a question for each hiding place, for example:

What is for lunch today? ......
How many pictures are there on the wall? ......

Alternatively, the clues could be written on cards of different colours, and the children have to tell you which clue was which colour.

Different teams could have clues in a different order, so that they do not cheat by following each other round.

4 Write or record the clues.

5 Hide the treasure. This should be a small item such as some dried fruit or some stationery. Remember that you need enough treasure for each child to get some.

6 Prepare a couple of 'spare clues' to use as practice examples.

IN CLASS

1 Draw a large chest on the board. Ask the children what it is and what might be in it. Get them to tell you what treasure is, who hides it, who finds it, and so on. Then introduce the idea of a treasure trail with clues.

2 Tell them that there is some treasure hidden in the school and that they are going to try and find it. You could show them a scruffy piece of paper with some clues on it (burning the edges creates a good effect).

3 Divide the class into four teams. Write a sample clue on the board, and tell each team to read it and tell you where the next clue will be. Do this with a few more sample clues, until they have got the idea of going from clue to clue.

4 Give the teams their clues or cassettes, and start the treasure hunt.

5 As the teams finish, check that they have been round all the clues.

FOLLOW-UP

If you have written the clues using a particular grammatical structure, focus on this, and then ask the children to draw a treasure map and write similar clues.

6.8 Body writing

LEVEL

1, 2

AGE

All

TIME

20 minutes

AIMS

Linguistic: to associate the spoken and written forms of letters/numbers/words.
Other: to build co-operation between the members of the groups.

DESCRIPTION

In groups or individually, the children make shapes, letters, numbers, or words with their bodies.

PREPARATION

None.

IN CLASS

1 Put the children into groups of five or six.

2 Explain that they are going to form letters with their bodies. They can stand up or lie down.

3 Start with simple letters or shapes which one child can make on his or own: for instance, I or T. Then go on to letters such as A or M, for which they have to co-operate.

4 Say the name of the letter and give them a minute or so to organize themselves. When they are ready, go round the groups saying which ones you think are really good and ask the other groups to look at them and say why.

The first time they do this activity you will probably have to give them some guidance.

5 Repeat the game several times with numbers and letters, and finally let each group make a number or letter that the others then try to guess.

VARIATION

Once the children are used to making letters you can ask them to make words.

6.9 All change

LEVEL

All

AGE GROUP

All

TIME

30 minutes +

AIMS

Linguistic: listening for detail, *It's got …*, *It's* + adjective, *It lives in …*, *It can …*.
Other: to develop a sense of group identity, general knowledge.

DESCRIPTION

The children stand in groups of four or five. Each group has a name. The teacher calls out the names of two of the groups and they change places.

PREPARATION

Decide what you are going to call the groups. You can use a wide range of topics (for example, monsters, shops, jobs), or any topic that the children have been studying at school.

IN CLASS

First play the simplest form of the game:

1 Divide children into groups of four or five, and give each group a name.

2 The groups stand around the edge of the gym or playground. When the teacher calls out the names of two of the groups they change places.

VARIATION 1

This is a more competitive version of the game.

1 One of the groups does not have a place, but stands in the middle of the gym or playground.

2 When the two groups you have named change places, the group in the middle tries to 'occupy' one of their places, and the group whose place they have taken has to go to the middle.

VARIATION 2

Do stages 1–3 in the classroom, then take the class to the playground or gym.

1 Elicit the names of some animals from the children.

2 When you have a dozen or so, say a few sentences about one of them and ask the children if they know which one it is. For example:

It's very big, it's grey, it's got very big ears.

This introduces the children to the idea of defining an animal by its size, colour, and characteristics.

3 Now divide the class into groups of four or five. Ask each group to think of a different animal and to write four or five sentences about it. You can give them sentence patterns such as:

It's + (colour), *it's* + (size), *it lives in …, it eats ….*

Collect each group's sentences in.

4 Each group finds a space round the edge of the gym and the game can start. Instead of simply calling out the animal names of two of the groups, call out the children's sentences, one sentence about one group and then another about another group, and so on. For example, if there are groups called 'Elephants' and 'Rabbits', the teacher can call out:

It's grey   *It's grey*
It's got two big ears   *It's got two long ears*
It likes bananas   *It likes carrots.*

The children listen, and when two groups recognize their animals, they change places.

7 Songs and chants

Music and rhythm are an essential part of language learning for young learners. Children really enjoy learning and singing songs, and older learners find working with current or well-known pop songs highly motivating.

We have all experienced songs which we just can't get out of our heads. Music and rhythm make it much easier to imitate and remember language than words which are 'just spoken'—if you teach children a song, it somehow 'sticks'.

A chant is like a song without music, or a poem with a very marked rhythm. There are many different songs and chants, from traditional ones to specially written material for young language learners. Traditional songs and chants often contain obscure or out-of-date language which may outweigh their usefulness, but they do have the advantage of being part of English-speaking culture.

Some songs are good for singing, others for doing actions to the music, and the best ones are good for both! You can use songs and chants to teach children the sounds and rhythm of English, to reinforce structures and vocabulary, or as Total Physical Response activities—but above all to have fun.

You can use a song or a chant at any stage in a lesson: for example, at the beginning to mark the change from the previous subject to English; in the middle of a lesson as a break from another, more concentrated activity; or at the end, to round a lesson off. Songs and chants can also help to create a sense of group identity.

Pop songs are usually best used in listening activities. You need to select the song you use with care. Is the language too difficult? Can you hear the words? Is the subject-matter suitable? Older children enjoy working with popular songs so much that they are willing to tackle difficult language, and will often sing along when the song is played.

You can also use songs as background music while the children are working quietly on another task—it is surprising how much they absorb unconsciously.

This chapter contains a very small selection of songs and chants to use in class. Some sources of more songs are listed in the Further Reading section. Another useful book is *Music and Song* in this series, which has a section on young learners, and a very comprehensive bibliography.

7.1 Action songs

LEVEL

All

AGE GROUP

A, B

TIME

10–20 minutes

AIMS

Linguistic: to associate actions with words, to internalize the sounds and rhythms of English.
Other: to develop a sense of rhythm, to enjoy the music, to give the children a chance to 'let off steam'.

DESCRIPTION

The children do actions as they listen to and sing songs.

MATERIALS

Song cassette and cassette player, or music and a musical instrument.

PREPARATION

Listen to the song and practise doing the actions yourself.

IN CLASS

These are some general guidelines for doing action songs in class.

1 Play or sing the song once or twice with the children just listening, so that they begin to absorb the tune and rhythm.

2 Now play or sing the song again and get them to clap the rhythm and/or hum the tune to the music.

3 Get them to join in the actions with you.

4 Ask them if they can tell you what the song means from the actions. Explain anything they don't understand.

5 Play the song again. The children join in with the actions, and sing along with the words if they wish.

FOLLOW-UP 1

You can give older children the words of the song, perhaps with gaps to fill in, or to illustrate

FOLLOW-UP 2

It is a good idea to get the children to make an ongoing song book to which they add new songs as they learn them.

COMMENTS

1 Listening and doing actions is the best way to exploit traditional songs where the words are often difficult to understand. The actions keep the children interested and give them a reason for listening.

2 The children may well want to sing the words too. This is fine if they want to, but do not force them if they are not ready.

EXAMPLES _____   ### Parts of the body

Head and shoulders, knees and toes (traditional)

Actions: the children touch the parts of the body in the song.

The Hokey Cokey (traditional)

The children stand in a big circle.

Words	Actions
You put your *right hand in	*Everyone puts their right hand into the circle*
Your *right hand out	*Everyone puts their right hand out of the circle*
In, out, in, out	*Everyone puts their right hand in and out*
Shake it all about	*Everyone shakes their right hand vigorously*
You do the hokey cokey	*Everyone holds their elbows and moves their hips to the music*
And you turn around	*Everyone turns round on the spot*
That's what it's all about.	*Everyone holds hands*

Chorus

Oh, the hokey cokey	*The whole circle moves into the centre*
Oh, the hokey cokey	*The whole circle moves out again*
Oh, the hokey cokey	*Everyone lets go of one another's hands*
Knees bend, arms stretch,	*Do these actions.*
clap your hands.	

*In other verses, substitute *left hand*, *right leg*, *left leg*, *whole self* (or other parts of the body). It is best not to let it go on too long, however.

Here we go round the mulberry bush (traditional)

Chorus

Here we go round the mulberry bush
The mulberry bush, the mulberry bush
Here we go round the mulberry bush
On a cold and frosty morning.

Verse 1

This is the way we *clean our teeth
*Clean our teeth, clean our teeth
This is the way we *clean our teeth
On a cold and frosty morning.

Repeat chorus.

* In other verses, substitute 'wash our face', 'brush our hair', 'put on our clothes', 'eat our breakfast', and so on.

Actions: In the chorus the children stand in a big circle holding hands and skip round in time to the music.

In the verses they mime the actions.

Counting songs

Ten little fingers (from *Wee Sing*)

One little, two little, three little fingers
Four little, five little, six little fingers
Seven little, eight little, nine little fingers
Ten fingers on my hands.

Ten little, nine little, eight little fingers
Seven little, six little, five little fingers
Four little, three little, two little fingers
One finger on my hands.

Actions: The children show the correct number of fingers as they listen to the song.

One man went to mow (traditional)

Photocopiable © Oxford University Press

Words	*Actions*
One man went to mow	*Hold up one finger, then make a mowing motion (as if cutting grass with a scythe)*
Went to mow a meadow	*Repeat the mowing motion*
One man and his dog	*Hold up one finger and then make a dog's head with your hand*
Woof, woof	*Open your fingers in time to the 'woof, woof'*
Went to mow a meadow.	*Make a mowing motion*

Two men went to mow	*Hold up two fingers, then make a mowing motion*
Went to mow a meadow	*Repeat the mowing motion*
Two men, one man and his dog	*Hold up two fingers and then make a dog's head with your hand*
Woof, woof	*Open your fingers in time to the 'woof, woof'*
Went to mow a meadow.	*Make a mowing motion*

And so on until:

Ten men went to mow
Went to mow a meadow
Ten men, nine men, eight men, seven men, six men, five men, four men, three men, two men, one man and his dog
Woof, woof
Went to mow a meadow.

VARIATIONS

Put in more appropriate words for your children, for example:

One boy/girl went to see, went to see a friend
or
One boy/girl went to ride, went to ride his/her bike.

Spelling songs

Bingo (traditional)

Before singing the song, practise the letters and claps. Write 'BINGO' on the board, and teach the children to chant the letters. Now rub one letter out. Get the children to clap the missing letter and spell the rest of the word, keeping to the same rhythm. Continue like this until they are only clapping.

First time:	B	I	N	G	O
Second time:	clap	I	N	G	O
Third time:	clap	clap	N	G	O
And so on until:					
Last time:	clap	clap	clap	clap	clap

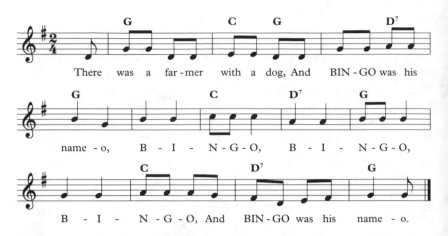

There was a farmer with a dog
And BINGO was his name-o
B—I—N—G—O
B—I—N—G—O
B—I—N—G—O
And BINGO was his name-o.

There was a farmer with a dog
And BINGO was his name-o
clap—I—N—G—O
clap—I—N—G—O
clap—I—N—G—O
And BINGO was his name-o.

Continue until the children are just clapping the letters of 'Bingo'.

Once the children know the words and the tune, you can substitute their names for 'Bingo'.

Songs for special occasions

Happy birthday (traditional)

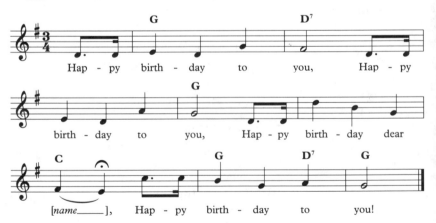

Happy birthday to you
Happy birthday to you
Happy birthday dear (name of the child)
Happy birthday to you!

Actions: The children sing and clap in time to the music. At the end of the song they do one clap for each year of the age of the birthday child.

Another way is to sing the song three times, starting very quietly and getting louder on each verse.

We wish you a Merry Christmas (traditional; adapted)

We wish you a Mer - ry Christ - mas, We wish you a Mer - ry Christ - mas, We wish you a Mer - ry Christ - mas, And a Hap - py New Year.

Chorus
We wish you a Merry Christmas
We wish you a Merry Christmas
We wish you a Merry Christmas
And a Happy New Year.

Let's all do a little *clapping
Let's all do a little *clapping
We wish you a Merry Christmas
And a Happy New Year.

Repeat chorus.

*Substitute stamping, waving, and so on in successive verses.

Actions: In the chorus the children form a 'snake' by holding onto one anothers' waists, and dance around the room, perhaps waving one hand.

In the verses the snake breaks up and the children clap (or stamp, or wave, etc.) in time to the music.

Ten little witches

This adaptation of 'Ten little fingers' (see above) can be sung at Hallowe'en.

Change 'fingers' to 'witches' and 'on my hands' to 'in the sky'. Give each child a number (from one to ten) and get them to squat in a row. When they hear their number they should stand up, and then when they hear it again they should squat down again. You could also make witches' hats for them to wear.

7.2 Poems, rhymes, and chants to say

LEVEL	**All**
AGE GROUP	**All**
TIME	**10–20 minutes**
AIMS	**Linguistic:** to practise the sounds, rhythms, and stress patterns of English, and in some cases to practise a structure. **Other:** to have fun, to feel a sense of achievement.
DESCRIPTION	The children learn and recite a poem, rhyme, or chant and, in some cases, do the actions to the words.
MATERIALS	Copies of the words (optional).
PREPARATION	Learn the poem yourself and practise saying it with a good beat. Add any actions you think are appropriate.
IN CLASS	These are some general guidelines for teaching a poem, rhyme, or chant. You would probably not do them all in one lesson!

1 Say the poem yourself, and demonstrate the actions.

2 See if the children can guess what it means.

3 Practise saying it with all the class, keeping up a good rhythm and listening out for pronunciation problems.

4 Teach the children the actions and get them to do them as you say the poem. It is not important if they do not all say the words at this stage.

5 (Optional) Write all or some of the poem on the board and explain any difficult words, or even translate it if you think necessary.

6 (Optional) Ask the children to look at the words on the board again, and rub out one or two words (you could substitute pictures). Get them to recite the poem, 'reading' the invisible words. Then rub out some more words and get them to recite it again. Go on like this until they are 'reading' the invisible poem.

7 The children say the words and do the actions.

FOLLOW-UP 1

As with songs, you can give the children the words to illustrate and get them to make a little book.

FOLLOW-UP 2

Get the children to change words in the poem, rhyme, or chant to make their own versions (see 'In a dark, dark wood' and 'A sailor went to sea', below). See also 4.4 and 4.5 for more ideas on how to get children to write their own poems in English.

COMMENTS

The best rhymes for language learning are repetitive ones in which just a few words change from verse to verse. Carolyn Graham's books on Jazz Chants are an excellent source of material. You will find more examples in the Further Reading section.

EXAMPLES

Five little elephants (adapted from *Of Frogs and Snails*)

Words	*Actions*
Five little elephants	*Five children stand in a row , using their arms as 'trunks'*
Standing in a row	
Five little trunks	
Waving hello	*The children wave hello with their trunks*
'Oh' said an elephant	*The first child looks at his or her watch, makes a surprised gesture, and hurries away*
'Time to go'	
Four little elephants	
Standing in a row.	

Continue with:
Four little elephants
Three little elephants
Two little elephants

And so on until
One little elephant
Standing in a row

One little trunk
Waving hello
'Oh' said the elephant
'Time to go!'
No little elephants
Standing in a row.

The Train
This chant should be said to the rhythm of a steam train moving
off slowly, gathering speed, and finally entering a tunnel with a
whistle. The stress on the words is vital, and is marked above
each one.

● . ● .
Coffee, coffee

● . ● . ● . ● .
Milk and sugar, milk and sugar

● . ● . ● . ● . ●
Strawberries and cream, strawberries and cream

● . ● . ● . ● . ● .
Chocolate cake and chocolate biscuits

● . ● . ● . ● . ●
Chocolate cake and chocolate biscuits

● . ●
Fish and chips

● . ●
Fish and chips

● . ●
Fish and chips

●
SOUP

●——
S-O-O-O-U-P

COMMENTS

1 As long as you keep the same rhythm, you can adapt this
chant to whatever food your children usually eat.

2 It is important that 'strawberries' and 'chocolate' are
pronounced as two syllables (i.e. with the first *e* and the second *o*
silent) in this chant.

In a dark, dark wood (traditional)

In a dark, dark wood there's a dark, dark house

In the dark, dark house there's a dark, dark cupboard

In the dark, dark cupboard there's a dark, dark shelf

On the dark, dark shelf there's a dark, dark box

And in the dark, dark box there's a ...

VARIATIONS

This poem can easily be changed by you or the children, for example:

In a big, big wood, there's a big, big castle
In the big, big castle there's a big, big room
In the big, big room, there's a big, big chest
In the big, big chest, there's a big, big key
The big, big key opens a big, big door
And behind the big, big door, there's a ...

FOLLOW-UP

Once the children have learned the poem they can illustrate it and imagine what's in the box.

A sailor went to sea (a traditional clapping rhyme)

A sailor went to sea, sea, sea

To see what he could see, see, see

But all that he could see, see, see

Was the bottom of the deep blue sea, sea, sea.

Actions: The children stand in pairs facing each other and clap in time to the rhythm marked above the words. The claps go like this:

First beat:	clap your own hands
Second beat:	clap your partner's right hand
Third beat:	clap your own hands
Fourth beat:	clap your partner's left hand
Fifth beat:	clap your own hands
Sixth, seventh, and eighth beats:	clap both your partner's hands three times (your right against his/her left and your left against his/her right).

VARIATIONS	You or the children can adapt this rhyme, though of course it is difficult to imitate the play on words. However, two or three rhyming couplets are just as good as long as you keep the same rhythm, for example:

My brother went to play, play, play
With all his friends one day, day, day
They all went to the park, park, park
And stayed there until dark, dark, dark.

7.3 Exploiting songs

LEVEL	**All**
AGE GROUP	**All**
TIME	**20–30 minutes**
AIMS	**Linguistic:** to practise listening skills, vocabulary, and in some cases a language point. **Other:** to enjoy the music, to introduce the children to aspects of English-speaking culture.
DESCRIPTION	Some ways of using songs in class: either songs specially written for learners, or songs written for native speakers.
MATERIALS	Cassettes and a cassette player; see individual activities.

Find the word

A very simple introductory activity to a song is to ask the children to listen for a certain word, and note down the number of times it occurs. For example, in the song 'Hello, goodbye' by the Beatles, you can ask the children to count the number of times they hear 'hello' and 'goodbye'.

More advanced learners can note down words with certain sounds in the song—for example, if your children have difficulty in hearing the difference between /i:/ and /ɪ/, you could ask them to write down words containing /i:/.

Song pictures 1

1 Choose a song which has a strong descriptive text. Find or draw a picture which illustrates it, but with some gaps or mistakes. Make copies for the children.

2 Give the children the copies of the picture. Ask them to listen to the song and complete or correct the picture.

Song pictures 2

You can use this technique with a song that tells a story.

1 Draw simple pictures to illustrate the story, cut them out, and make a worksheet with the pictures out of order.

2 Ask the children to listen to the song and put the pictures in order.

Gap fill songs

Choose a song which has clear words. Use any of the activities in 4.1, 'Variations on a gap'.

Mixed-up lines

1 Copy out the words of the song. Stick them onto card and cut them out. Mix up the order of the lines.

2 Ask the children to listen to the song and put the lines in the correct order.

This is especially effective with pop songs.

With a long song it is better to cut it into verses.

Song translations

1 Translate the song line by line into the children's native language, then mix up the lines.

2 Make copies and give the children one each, with a copy of the English words. Put them in pairs and ask them to match the lines.

COMMENTS

Many English pop songs are well known, even to the youngest learners, especially the theme songs to films or television series. Although the language is difficult, children will love using them in class. You could probably use at least two of the activities here in order to get the most out of each song.

8 Creative Activities

Creative activities and crafts are an important part of the general curriculum, as they not only stimulate children's imagination, but also develop skills such as hand-eye co-ordination. They are also very enjoyable and motivating. You can use them as an opportunity to give instructions in English, or you can use what the children make for other language activities: for example, 8.10, 'Making books', with storytelling and writing; 8.5, 'Spinners', can be used for games; 8.4, 'Make a weather clock', can be used for an information gap activity; and 8.7, 'Making puppets' and 8.9, 'Making masks' for drama.

When you are planning a creative activity, it is essential that you try it out yourself first. Although I have tried to anticipate pitfalls, there may be some I have not discovered!

Don't expect works of art from your children—you may well get some, but always keep in mind that it is the *process* that is important, and the language used. It is unrealistic to expect the children to speak in English all the time they are working, though you should encourage them to use phrases such as *Can I have the scissors?* or *Do you like it?* You should use as much English as you can as the context will usually make your meaning clear. This is an excellent opportunity for some real communication in English, which should not be missed. If you play a tape of songs in English for the children to work to, you will be surprised how much goes in subconsciously.

When the children have finished, try and put on a display of what they have made, either in the classroom or around the school. This gives the children pride in their work, and other groups come into contact with English too.

More sources of craft activities in English are given in the Further Reading section. You will find other ideas which you can adapt in children's books and magazines in their own language.

8.1 Milly and Molly and the Big, Bad Cat

LEVEL	1
AGE GROUP	**A, B**
TIME	**Three slots: 20 minutes, 30 minutes, and 20 minutes (either all together or in separate lessons)**

AIMS

Linguistic: listening to a story.
Other: colouring, cutting out, and sticking.

DESCRIPTION

The teacher tells the children a story using cut-out figures. The children then make their own figures and use them to act out the story.

MATERIALS

Figures of Milly, Molly, and the Big, Bad Cat (see Worksheets 8.1a and b at the end of the book), string (optional), glue, scissors, coloured pencils, some yellow plasticine to represent the cheese.

PREPARATION

1 Make a set of figures of Milly, Molly, and the Big, Bad Cat for yourself, and stick them on card.

2 Read through the story outline (see below) and practise telling it. Remember to use lots of expression, mime, and repetition.

3 Make a copy of Worksheets 8.1a and b for each child. If you can't make copies, make some templates in strong card for the children to draw round.

STORY OUTLINE

MILLY AND MOLLY AND THE BIG, BAD CAT

Once upon a time—two mice—Milly and Molly—friends
One day—very hungry
Suddenly—smelt something—cheese!
But—problem—Big, Bad Cat was guarding the cheese!
Milly had an idea—crept out of the hole—made a rude face at the cat.
Big, Bad Cat was very angry—said 'Miaow'—ran after Milly.
Milly ran and ran and ran.
Meanwhile—Molly crept out—took the cheese!
Milly ran and ran—just got back to the hole in time.
They ate the cheese.
Big, Bad Cat said 'Miaow'.

IN CLASS

Part One

1 If you can, get the children to sit around you in a circle so that the Big, Bad Cat can run round the outside after Milly.

2 Show the children the figures you have made. Put Milly and Molly in their hole—perhaps under a chair—and the cheese in the middle of the circle.

3 Tell the story twice. The first time the children just listen, but the second time ask them the names of the animals and encourage them to mime with you.

4 Ask for volunteers for each of the animals and tell the story again, this time with the children acting it out.

Part Two (This can be in the next lesson.)

5 Show the children how to cut out the figures, colour them, fold them, and stick them together. If you wish, they can stick on string 'tails'. As they are working, go round the class praising their work and asking them questions such as *What colour is the cat?*

Part Three (This can be in the next lesson.)

6 Put the children into groups of three and tell them to decide who is going to be Milly, Molly, and the Big, Bad Cat. Give each group a piece of plasticine (for cheese). Then tell them to find a space to work in, decide where Milly and Molly live, and put the cheese in its place.

7 Tell the story again. The children act it out while you tell it.

FOLLOW-UP 1

The children draw one of the scenes of the story and tell you the caption they want to give it. You translate it into English and they copy the words on to their picture.

FOLLOW-UP 2

The children make a book of the story (see 8.10, 'Making books').

FOLLOW-UP 3

The children make masks of the characters and act out the story (see 8.9, 'Making masks'). More advanced children could invent a dialogue.

FOLLOW-UP 4

The children invent another story using the same characters.

COMMENTS

1 Choose follow-up activities carefully, depending on the children's age and how much they enjoy the story. Do not use the same story too many times.

2 You will find other ideas for these kinds of stories in cartoons and comic strips.

3 An excellent aid to storytelling is a felt board. If you stick pieces of velcro to the back of the figures you, or the children, can move them around at will.

8.2 Vocabulary jigsaws

LEVEL   1, 2

AGE GROUP   A, B

TIME   30 minutes

AIMS   **Linguistic:** to revise vocabulary.
Other: to practise drawing, colouring, cutting, and sticking; to practise matching pieces of a jigsaw.

DESCRIPTION   The children complete a jigsaw framework with words and pictures, cut it out, and remake the jigsaw.

MATERIALS   One jigsaw you have already made, blu-tack, copies of the empty jigsaw for the children (see Worksheet 8.2 at end of book), thin card (optional), an envelope for each child, coloured pencils, glue, scissors.

PREPARATION   Make a jigsaw yourself. If you have a large class, it is a good idea to make a giant jigsaw on a sheet of card. Stick it on the board so that everyone can see it.

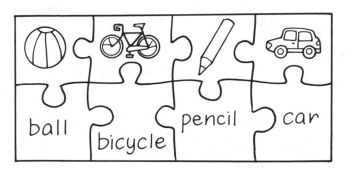

IN CLASS   1 Show the children the picture pieces of your jigsaw and ask them the English words for what is on the pictures. Stick them on the board or put them on a table where everyone can see them.

2 Show the children the word pieces and get them to match them to the pictures. Then ask for volunteers to put all the pieces together to make the whole jigsaw.

3 Explain that they are going to make a similar jigsaw. If the children are very young, they should copy your pictures and words. If they are older, let the class decide what topic they want to work on, and let each child choose his or her own words and pictures.

4 Give out the blank jigsaws and check that the children understand what they are going to do.

5 While the children are working, go round the class
encouraging, commenting, and asking simple questions such as
What's in this picture? or *How do you say this in English?*

6 (Optional) Before they cut out their jigsaw, give them a piece
of card to stick it onto—the pieces will be easier to fit together
and will last much longer. Give each child an envelope to keep
the pieces in, and tell them to write their name and the topic of
the jigsaw on it.

7 As the children finish, get them to swap jigsaws and to try to
do one another's.

8.3 Pick up twos (pelmanism)

LEVEL	**All**
AGE GROUP	**All**
TIME	**30 minutes to make the cards, 15–20 minutes to play the game.**
AIMS	**Linguistic:** Depends on the cards made. **Other:** to exercise the memory.
DESCRIPTION	The children make a set of cards that form pairs (see below for types of pairs). They use these cards to play pick up twos (pelmanism).
MATERIALS	A set of demonstration cards, eight playing-card-sized pieces of card for each child, envelopes, coloured pencils, or pictures from magazines, and glue.
PREPARATION	1 Decide which language features you want to practise.

2 Make a set of four or five pairs of cards that you can use to
demonstrate the game. If you have a large class, these should be
big cards that you can stick on the board for all the children to
see. They should all be the same size, with one side blank and
one with pictures or words. If you are not good at drawing, you
can use pictures from magazines. You can mark the back of the
cards, or use two colours, in order to distinguish word cards
from picture cards.

Types of pairs

Vocabulary

One card has a picture and the other the corresponding word.
or
Both cards have pictures and the children name them out loud as
they turn them over.

Sentences

One card has a picture and the other the corresponding sentence.

Question and answer

One card has a question and the other the answer.

Opposites

The pairs are made up of opposites.

Verbs

One card has the infinitive, the other the simple past form or past participle—or you can make the game pick-up-threes and include all three parts of the verb.

Free association

For more advanced learners. The cards are not in fixed pairs, but can show words, pictures, or both. The children turn over any two cards; if they can make an English sentence using what is on both cards, they can keep the pair.

IN CLASS

Part One

1 Show the class your cards, and ask for volunteers to put them into pairs.

2 How to play:
Stick the cards on the board face down, putting the word cards on one side and the picture cards on the other. Ask a child to turn one of each over. If they match, he or she keeps them and has another turn. If not, he or she must turn them back again and another child has a turn. As this is a memory game it is very important that the cards are never moved, only turned over and back.

3 When they have got the idea of the game, tell them that they are going to make some cards themselves. Explain what they have to do (this depends on the kind of pairs you have decided to use), give out the pieces of card, and let them start.

4 As the children work, go round the class commenting, praising, and helping where necessary.

5 When they finish, give them an envelope to keep their cards in.

Part Two (This can be in another lesson.)

6 Put the children in groups of four. They should pool their cards and play the game (see Stage 2).

7 The winner is the player with the most pairs.

8.4 Make a weather clock

LEVEL	**1, 2**
AGE GROUP	**A, B**
TIME	**30 minutes**
AIMS	**Linguistic:** weather vocabulary, to follow spoken instructions. **Other:** drawing, colouring, and cutting, and to think about designing symbols.
DESCRIPTION	The children make a 'weather clock' with movable hands that they can set according to the day's weather.
MATERIALS	A weather clock you have made, photocopies of the blank clock for the children (see Worksheet 8.4 at end of book), strips of card for the 'hands', a split pin for each child.
PREPARATION	1 Make a weather clock yourself:

a Draw weather symbols on the 'clock'.

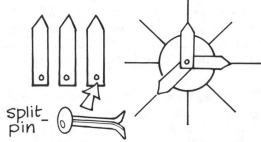

b Cut out 'hands' of thin card and pin them in the middle.

2 Think about how you will give the children their instructions.

3 Make a copy of the blank clock for each child (see Worksheet 8.4).

4 Cut out strips of card for the hands of the clocks.

IN CLASS 1 Ask the children to name different sorts of weather in English, using mime to help them, and make a list on the board.

2 Ask for a volunteer to come and draw a picture on the board to represent one of the kinds of weather on the list. Start with something easy to draw, like *sunny*, and then go on to something more difficult, like *windy*.

If they are not sure what to draw, ask them questions such as *What do trees do when it is windy? And the leaves? And your umbrella? And your hat?*

3 Show them your weather clock and ask *What's the weather like today?* Set the hands according to their answer.

4 Tell them that they are each going to make a clock, and tell them what to do, demonstrating at the same time. Give out the worksheets.

COMMENTS

Another way of presenting the idea of symbols is to get the children to look at the symbols used in weather charts on the television or in newspapers.

When the clocks are finished you can use them in a number of ways:

FOLLOW-UP 1

As the basis for an information gap activity. The children work in pairs: one child sets the hand of his or her clock out of sight of the other, the other child asks questions until he or she can set the hands of his or her clock to the same kind of weather.

FOLLOW-UP 2

As a listening activity: you talk about the weather and the children set the hands of their clocks according to what they hear.

FOLLOW-UP 3

Put the clocks on the wall (or let the children take them home) and set the hands correctly each day.

VARIATIONS

You can use the 'clock' idea for other topics:
Illnesses: *He's got a cold, a headache, or toothache.*
Feelings: *I'm happy, sad, or angry.*
Clothes: *I'm wearing trousers, a shirt, and a jumper.*

8.5 Spinners

LEVEL

All

AGE GROUP

All

TIME

30 minutes to make the spinners, 10–20 minutes to play a game.

AIMS

Linguistic: reading and following instructions in English.
Other: using a pair of compasses, colouring, and cutting.

DESCRIPTION

The children make spinners that can be used in a number of games—there are some suggestions below.

MATERIALS

Card, pairs of compasses or some hexagonal templates, cocktail sticks (or used matches or short pencils), scissors, coloured pencils, envelopes.

PREPARATION

1 Decide which of the games you want the children to make.

2 Make a spinner yourself to illustrate the game.

3 Younger children will not be able to make their own hexagons, so make templates for them to draw round, or photocopies to cut out and stick on card.

IN CLASS

1 Show the children the spinner you have made and demonstrate the game. Draw the diagrams on the board as you go.

2 Show the children how to draw a hexagon:

a Set the compasses at about 3 cm and draw a circle.

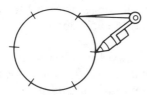

b Keep the compasses at the same setting and put the point of the compasses at any point on the circle. Draw small pencil marks around the circle.

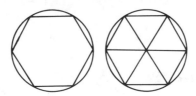

c Then join up the marks to make a hexagon. Cut out the hexagon and draw lines across it to make six triangles.

3 When all the children have made a hexagon, tell them how to play the game. Answer any questions they may have.

4 Give each child an envelope to keep their spinner in.

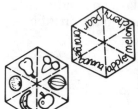

Games with spinners

Vocabulary match

The children work in pairs. One makes a spinner with pictures and the other makes a spinner with the corresponding words. They take it in turns to spin both spinners together. If the word and the picture are the same, they win a point.

Spinner lotto

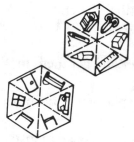

The children play in groups of three or four. Each child makes a spinner with pictures only. Then each child makes a list of six of any of the items on all the spinners. The children take turns to spin their spinners, and if the picture is the same as a word on their list, they cross it off. The first child to cross off all his or her words is the winner.

Collect a set

The teacher writes groups of words from six word families on the board, for example: 'The family', 'Animals', 'The house', 'Clothes', 'Food and Drink', and 'Colours'. Each child must draw one item from each word family on his or her spinner.

The children work in groups of four to play the game. Each child decides which word family to collect, and takes it in turns to spin all four spinners. The first child to collect four words in his or her word family is the winner.

Board games

You can use spinners instead of dice in board games (for example, 6.5). Each triangle has a number, a colour, or a word from the board game.

8.6 Twin plasticine monsters

LEVEL	2
AGE GROUP	**All**
TIME	**30 minutes**
AIMS	**Linguistic:** parts of the body, colours, giving and understanding spoken descriptions. **Other:** to develop modelling skills.
MATERIALS	Plasticine in different colours.

DESCRIPTION

The children each make a monster out of plasticine and then describe it to their partner, who has to try and make one the same.

PREPARATION

1 Make a plasticine monster yourself.

2 Make sure that there is enough plasticine for each child to have four or five different colours.

IN CLASS

1 Draw a monster on the board and check that the children know the English names of parts of the body and how to describe the monster—for example, *He's got a long tail.*

2 Show the children your plasticine monster and get them to describe it in English.

3 Put the children in pairs and give out the plasticine. Each pair should have the same colours.

4 Tell them all to use half of their plasticine to make a monster, but not to let their partner see it. (They will use the other half later to make a replica of their partner's monster.) Put a time limit on this step or the monsters will be too complicated!

5 Now tell one of the children in each pair to describe their monster in English to their partner (still not letting them see it), so that the partner can make a 'twin'. When they have finished they should compare monsters, then swap roles.

6 When all the monsters are finished, the children can give them names and display them in a 'monster park'.

FOLLOW-UP 1

Use the twin monsters to practise comparisons—for example, *Timmy Monster's nose is longer than Tommy Monster's.*

FOLLOW-UP 2

One child describes a monster from the 'monster park' and the others guess which one it is.

FOLLOW-UP 3

Use the monsters to make up a story.

VARIATION

The children could draw monsters instead of modelling them. See also 2.2, 'On the farm'.

COMMENTS

Make it clear that the aim of the game is to describe the monster so well that their partner's monster looks just like theirs. Sometimes children think they have 'won' if their partner *can't* make one like theirs.

8.7 Making puppets

LEVEL	**All**
AGE GROUP	**All**
TIME	**20–40 minutes**
AIMS	**Linguistic:** following written or spoken instructions. Using the puppets gives speaking practice. **Other:** to develop manual dexterity, co-ordination, and co-operation.
MATERIALS	See the different types of puppet (below).
PREPARATION	1 Always make a puppet yourself before doing it with your class. 2 Decide how you are going to give the instructions to the children (written or orally).

Finger puppets

MATERIALS
Thin felt tip pens, coloured pencils, scissors, circles of paper, the children's fingers!

IN CLASS

1 The children colour the paper circle to represent the puppet's clothes.

2 They cut out the circle and make a small cut in the centre for the neck.

They make a cut from the edge of the circle to the centre.

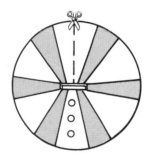

3 They draw a face on one of their fingers and put the circle over the finger, overlapping the paper at the cut to make a 'skirt' shape.

Stick puppets

MATERIALS
A copy of Worksheet 8.7 (see end of book) for each child, two thin sticks for each puppet, coloured pencils, scissors, card, glue, a split pin for each puppet, sticky tape.

IN CLASS

1 The children colour the figure and the arm on Worksheet 8.7. They stick them onto card and cut them out.

2 Then they join the arm to the rest of the figure at the elbow with the split pin, and stick one thin stick on to the back of the puppet and one on to the arm with sticky tape.

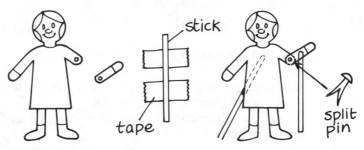

Paper bag puppets

MATERIALS

A paper bag for each child, coloured pencils, scissors, glue, wool for the hair (optional), an elastic band for each child.

IN CLASS

1 The children draw a face on the paper bag. Alternatively, they could stick on cut-out eyes, nose, and mouth, and wool for hair.

2 When the face is ready they put it over their fist and fix it on their wrist with an elastic band.

COMMENTS

1 As well as these puppets that the children make, it is useful to have some other, more sophisticated ones which you yourself use in class, for example glove puppets or pop-up puppets. If you speak the children's native language and have trouble establishing 'English only time', you can tell the children that the puppets only speak English. You can use them for general warm-up chat, giving instructions, or introducing language.

2 Children really enjoy using puppets, and they often motivate the most reticent child to speak.

8.8 Growing seeds

LEVEL	2, 3
AGE GROUP	B, C
TIME	5–10 minutes a day for 2 weeks, then 5–10 minutes a week for 4–6 weeks
AIMS	**Linguistic:** to follow instructions in English, to keep a written record of a process. **Other:** to encourage observation over a period of time, to practise measuring, to reinforce what the children learn in science lessons.
DESCRIPTION	The children plant bean seeds in a jar and observe the bean as it germinates and the plant as it grows.
MATERIALS	A jam jar for each child, two or three bean seeds for each child, enough blotting paper to put in all the jars, water, copies of the instructions and record sheets (see Worksheets 8.8a and b at the end of the book).
PREPARATION	1 If you have time, follow the instructions yourself first. 2 Tell the children to bring an empty jam jar each to school. 3 Either buy some dried beans or tell the children to bring two or three each. 4 Make a photocopy of the instructions and record sheet for each child. If you can't make copies, write the instructions on a large poster, and draw the record sheet grid on the board for the children to copy.
IN CLASS	1 Show the children a bean seed. Ask them what it is, and tell them that they are going to plant some and watch them grow. Teach them basic vocabulary such as *seed, root, shoot, leaf/leaves, water, plant* (v), and *grow* (v), as well as words they need to understand in the instructions. 2 Give out the instructions and record sheets and ask the children to read 'Day 1'. Check that they understand and then let them start. 3 Set aside five or ten minutes in the following lessons for the children to continue with the activity: every day at first, then once a week.

When the root, seed leaves, and then the true leaves appear, the children will probably need help in filling in the record sheet. You can give them some model sentences, or some questions to answer. When the plants are about ten centimetres tall, the children can take them home and transplant them to a pot or into the ground. They can continue recording their progress if they want to.

FOLLOW-UP

Older children can do other experiments with the plants, for example, to see what happens when one plant is kept in the light and another in the dark, or whether adding liquid fertilizer makes any difference to growth.

COMMENTS

1 It is always a good idea to be aware of what the children are studying in science.

2 Germinate a few spare beans yourself, as some will not grow.

VARIATION

You can also do other science activities in English, for example, measuring shadows at different times of day. For more ideas, see the Further Reading section.

8.9 Making masks

LEVEL

All

AGE GROUP

All

TIME

30 minutes

AIMS

Linguistic: following spoken or written instructions.
Other: to encourage creativity, to motivate the children to speak.

DESCRIPTION

The children make masks, which they can use to practise speaking English.

MATERIALS

Coloured pencils, scissors, glue, wool, pictures from magazines—see the different types of mask.

PREPARATION

1 Always try making the mask yourself first.

2 Decide how you are going to give the instructions (spoken or written).

IN CLASS   **Paper plate masks**

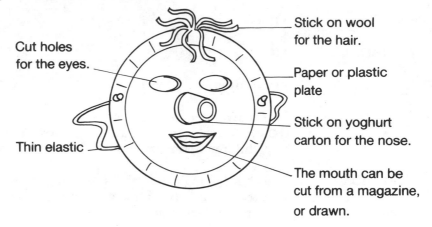

Cut holes
for the eyes.

Stick on wool
for the hair.

Paper or plastic
plate

Stick on yoghurt
carton for the nose.

Thin elastic

The mouth can be
cut from a magazine,
or drawn.

Paper bag masks

head-sized
strong paper
bag

Stick on wool
for the hair.

Cut holes to
see through

Eyes, ears, nose,
mouth, etc. can
be cut from
magazines or
drawn.

A mask on a stick

1 Draw a 25 cm circle on card
and cut it out.

3 Thread string through the hole
and pull it tight to curve the
mask round
(optional).   **Back**

Front

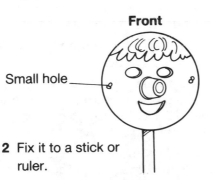

Small hole

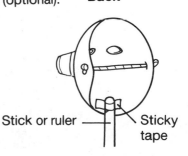

2 Fix it to a stick or
ruler.

Stick or ruler

Sticky
tape

COMMENTS   Children love dressing up, and masks are a powerful aid to
assuming another, often less inhibited, personality. You can use
them in almost any speaking activity, and in drama.

8.10 Making books

LEVEL	**All**
AGE GROUP	**All**
TIME	**30 minutes +**
AIMS	**Linguistic:** depends on the book. **Other:** to make children aware of books and book making, to help children appreciate books, to stimulate creativity.
DESCRIPTION	The children make books of their own. These can be based on a topic such as 'My family' or 'My day', stories (see 4.6), or projects—in fact almost anything.
MATERIALS	Paper, thin card for the cover, coloured pencils, scissors, glue, a stapler or blunt needles and thread—see the different types of book.
PREPARATION	1 Make examples of a book at various stages of production— cut-out pages, written pages ready for binding, the cover, and the finished book. 2 It is a good idea to make a poster or worksheets showing the different stages of the process. The children can refer to them instead of always coming to you.
IN CLASS	If you are making books as one of a series of lessons on a theme, the children can help to decide the content of their books. If the book making itself is the main focus of the lesson, you will need to give the children clear guidelines on content. Adapt the following steps to suit your situation. 1 Ask the pupils (in their first language if necessary) to tell you the essential features of a book: for example, pages, cover, title, author, numbers on the pages. The older the children are, the more detailed the description should be. 2 Explain that they are going to make a book themselves. Show them the one you have made. 3 Explain how to make the book, demonstrating the steps and referring to the poster or worksheet as you go. If you are working with younger children, it is better to explain a step and let them do it before going on to the next step. 4 As the children work, go round the class monitoring, encouraging, and sorting out difficulties, but refer them to the poster or worksheet, or to each other, whenever you can. 5 When they finish the books, encourage them to look at one another's. You could also make a display on the wall.

Types of book

A traditional book

1 Make cover out of card. It should be a bit bigger than the pages.

2 Cut pages out of white or coloured paper.

3 Remember to leave a margin when you write on them.

4 Staple or sew the pages into the cover.

If you are going to keep adding pages, punch holes in them and tie them in with string or ribbon.

The book can be tall and thin, or short and fat —whatever seems suitable for the topic.

A film strip book

1 Cut a strip of card (the film) and divide it into squares (for 'photos').

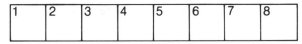

2 Write the text and draw the pictures in the squares—from right to left.

3 Cut another piece of card, just over twice as wide as the first.

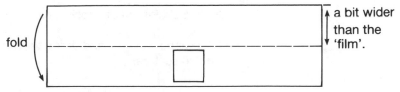

fold — a bit wider than the 'film'.

Cut out a square a bit smaller than one 'photo'.

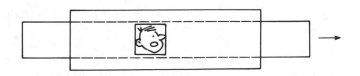

A concertina book

1 Take a long sheet of paper and fold it in a zig-zag.

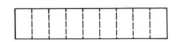

2 Write the text on the inside pages, using the two ends as the covers. You can stick card on these.

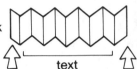

3 Fold the book together and, if you like, hold it together with a paper clip.

Note: You can cut simple shapes out of the zigzag-folded paper to suit your theme. For example 'My friends' could be simple people, shapes, etc.

A flap book

1 Make the pages and cover in the same way as for a traditional book.

2 Draw a picture with a hidden object in it.

3 Draw a flap to cover it. Cut it out.

4 Stick the flap on the picture using clear tape as a hinge.

A circular book

1 Cut two circles out of strong paper.

2 Cut a window in one, and divide the other into 6–8 sectors.

3 Write or draw in the sectors.

4 Pin the 'window' circle on top of the 'text' circle.

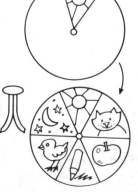

You can use this kind of book for writing about daily routines, or topics.

9 Video

Video and television form a part of many children's lives nowadays, and can also be a very useful tool in the language classroom. However, there is a big difference between watching television at home for relaxation and watching a video in a lesson, where the teacher devises activities and tasks that encourage the children to interact with the video and learn from it.

Videos provide a ready-made context for the presentation of new vocabulary, structures, and functions, as well as providing a stimulus for speaking. They can also provide an excellent source of input for topic-based work. By combining spoken language with images, videos parallel real life. The visuals help children to understand the situation and therefore the language—for example, beginners hearing *Come here* on an audio cassette are unlikely to understand it, but if they see it on a video accompanied by a gesture and response, the meaning is immediately obvious. It is this aspect that we need to exploit when preparing video tasks.

You can use both authentic videos, recorded from television (but please take your country's copyright rules into account), or videos that have been specially designed for children learning English. Criteria to bear in mind when selecting a video are:

– the kind of video: when using authentic videos make sure they have a high visual content, for example cartoons, short stories, advertisements, or educational programmes, rather than 'talking heads' in debates and discussions;

– length: it is better to select a short sequence (5 to 10 minutes) and exploit it to the full, than to spend a whole lesson passively watching a long video;

– the language level: videos made for EFL use graded language, but authentic videos often contain complicated and colloquial language. When using an authentic video, make sure that there is as much visual support as possible and that the tasks do not require the children to understand slang or unusual expressions.

When preparing a video lesson, just as with any other lesson, it is essential that you have a clear aim in mind: for example, presenting new language or complementing your textbook. Always keep in mind the basic principles of starting with 'easy' tasks to give the children the gist of the video, then moving to more demanding tasks that provide new language or opportunities for language practice (see 9.1, 'Making the most of a video'). When you prepare worksheets of your own, try them out with a colleague before using them in class if you can.

Making videos

Making videos is highly motivating. It gives the children an opportunity to use their language resources, and also encourages them to work together to achieve a group or class product. The process of making the video is an opportunity for the children to use English, especially in a multilingual class.

Videoing the children in an activity like 9.3, 'Act out a scene', greatly improves their performance.

Older children can learn how to manipulate a video camera, but with young children it is best for the teacher, another adult, or an older child to be the cameraperson.

For more ideas on using and making videos, I recommend *Video* by Richard Cooper, Mike Lavery, and Mario Rinvolucri, in this series.

9.1 Making the most of a video

LEVEL	**All**
AGE GROUP	**All**
TIME	**15–30 minutes**
AIMS	**Linguistic:** to develop listening skills, to present and practise new language and vocabulary, to develop awareness of non-linguistic communication such as facial expressions, gestures, and body language.
DESCRIPTION	Some basic ideas on how to exploit a video.
MATERIALS	Video player and cassette.
PREPARATION	1 Select a short video clip appropriate for your children (see chapter introduction).

2 Prepare the tasks. You will need:

– a first viewing task that introduces the children to the video
– one or more tasks to help the children understand
– possibly a language task
– a follow-up task.

See below for ideas.

3 Make copies of the task sheets, or make posters with the tasks on them.

EXAMPLES   **First viewing**

First viewing tasks should be very simple. Their aim is to give the children a reason for watching the video, and familiarize them with it.

– Ask the children to watch the video and tell you how many characters there are, and their names if possible.

– Cover the video, or turn it round, or turn down the picture. The children listen to the soundtrack and guess where the story takes place, who the characters are, and possibly what is happening.

– Write three or four very basic comprehension questions on the board for the children to answer after watching.

– If you use a video with a story line, for example *Muzzy*, ask the children to recall the previous episode and to predict what is going to happen. Then they watch and see if they were right. You can help them by giving them alternatives to choose from.

Further comprehension

These tasks should help the children understand the video in more detail, and should focus on both the language and the pictures. It is important that the language of the task helps the children make sense of what they are hearing, and reinforces the visual aspect of the video.

– The children answer true/false questions on the story.

– Give the children simple sentences that tell the story, but out of order. The children put them in the right order.

– Write on the board five key phrases from the video and a few which are not in it. The children watch and tell you which ones they hear.

– Write three summaries of the story, one of which is correct. The children choose the correct summary.

– Write out the story with some incorrect details, and read it to the children. They try to spot the mistakes, and possibly correct them.

– If the video has a sound-track with sound-effects rather than dialogue, you can cover the video before putting it on, or turn the picture down. Pause after each sound and ask the children to discuss what is happening in groups. Alternatively, you can give them a number of possibilities to choose from.

Language tasks

These should focus the children's attention on a point of language, for example a structure, a function, or even intonation patterns.

– Pause the video after an example of the language point you want to focus on, and ask the children what the person in the video said and what it means. If the language point is repeated throughout the video, after the children have heard it a few times you can stop the tape before an example and ask the children to predict what is going to be said.

– Give the children a few key phrases from the video. The children identify who says what, and then in what order.

Follow-up tasks

Follow-up tasks should build on the language and/or topic of what the children have been watching. You can do them immediately after the video, or in the next lesson.

– Give the children a situation in which they could use the language from the video. For example, if the video is about restaurant language, set up a restaurant role play or do 3.5, 'At a restaurant'.

– The children draw a picture of a scene from the video, or make a book telling the story. Alternatively, you can draw the scene with empty speech bubbles, and the children write what the characters say.

– The children make puppets to represent the characters in the video and dramatize a scene. See 8.7, 'Making puppets'.

9.2 Spot the items

LEVEL	**All**
AGE GROUP	**All**
TIME	**20 minutes**
AIMS	**Linguistic:** to reinforce vocabulary. **Other:** to encourage accurate observation.
DESCRIPTION	The children look for items in a video.
MATERIALS	Video player, video cassette, list of items.
PREPARATION	**1** Choose a video clip about five minutes long, which shows a variety of objects. Watch the video a couple of times and make a list of between five and ten items for the children to look out for. Choose some obvious things and some others that are more hidden.
	2 Copy the words on to a worksheet and make photocopies for the children, or write them on a poster or the board.
IN CLASS	**1** Let the children watch the video once.

2 Show them the list of items, and check that they know all the words. Explain that they have to watch the video again and look for the items.

3 (Optional) Tell the children to turn their worksheets over, or cover up the word list as they watch the video.

4 The children work in pairs and note down the words they see.

5 Let them watch the video again and check their list.

6 Play the video again: this time the children stop you when they see a word on the list, and tell you what it is.

FOLLOW-UP	Ask the children in which order they saw the things, to practise *first, second, third, before,* and *after.*
VARIATION	For older children, you can also think of items that are not in the video, and some misleading ones: for example, 'a big hat' if the hat in the video is small.
COMMENTS	*Wizadora* contains a number of unusual objects (see Further Reading).

9.3 Act out a scene

LEVEL	2, 3
AGE GROUP	B, C
TIME	**45 minutes**
AIMS	**Linguistic:** to practise speaking. **Other:** to develop dramatic techniques such as gestures and facial expressions.
DESCRIPTION	The children identify sentences in the video, then use them to act out what they have seen.
MATERIALS	Video player, video cassette, copies of speech bubbles (see Preparation), 'props' (optional).
PREPARATION	**1** Choose a 5–10 minute video clip with a dialogue that includes language you want to work on. Pick out some phrases for the children to focus on: five or six if the language is new, eight to ten if the children have already come across the language. **2** Draw speech bubbles on a piece of paper, and write the phrases from the dialogue in them, but not in the order in which they come in the video. Make a copy for each child.

3 (Optional) Ask the children to bring in some clothes or objects ('props') to use when acting.

IN CLASS

1 Play the video clip once and let the children simply watch it—this first contact is important so that they get the gist of the story and enjoy watching the video.

2 Give out the sheets with the speech bubbles and give them a few minutes to read them. Make sure they understand the gist of the phrases.

3 Play the video again, and explain that they should number the speech bubbles in the order in which they hear them. Get them to compare their answers in pairs.

Alternatively, give each child a bubble and get them to stand up, or put up their hand, when they hear their phrase. Then put all the bubbles on the board in the right order, so that all the children can see them.

4 Check that all the children understand all the phrases.

5 Now play the video clip again. Pause the video after each phrase and ask them to repeat it all together.

6 Play the video clip again. Pause the video when you get to the key phrases. Get the children to say the words from the right speech bubble.

7 Finally, ask them to act the whole scene without the support of the video (using actions and words). Let them rehearse first, then each group performs to the rest of the class. Of course it need not be exactly the same as the video.

COMMENTS

If you have the facilities, you can video the children—this certainly improves their performance!

9.4 Back-to-back

LEVEL

3

AGE GROUP

C

TIME

20 minutes +

AIMS

Linguistic: to practise speaking, and listening for information.
Other: to develop co-operation between the children.

DESCRIPTION

The children work in pairs: one with their back to the video, the other facing it. The one who can see the video describes what he or she can see while the other uses this information to complete a task.

MATERIALS   Video player, video cassette, copies of the tasks (see
                             Preparation).

PREPARATION   1 Choose a short video clip with plenty of action which your
                             children will be able to describe in English.

                             2 Prepare a task for the children who will not see the video, for
                             example one of the comprehension tasks in 9.1, 'Making the
                             most of your video'. The task should be fairly simple.

                             3 Try out the activity with a colleague.

IN CLASS   1 Pre-teach any essential vocabulary.

                             2 Put the children in pairs so that only one of each pair can see
                             the video. Tell them who the characters are and what the video is
                             about.

                             3 Give the children with their backs to the video their tasks, and
                             give them time to read them.

                             4 Meanwhile, explain to the others that they must describe the
                             video to their partner in as much detail as possible.

                             5 Play the video once. The children who can see it just watch,
                             and the children who cannot see just listen.

                             6 Play the video again, this time pausing often for the children
                             who can see it to describe what they see.

                             7 The children with their backs to the video ask their partners
                             questions to find the answers to their tasks.

                             8 Finally, let all the children see the video and check their
                             answers.

                             9 Repeat the activity with a different video in another lesson,
                             with the roles reversed.

9.5 Film a dialogue

LEVEL   3

AGE GROUP   C

TIME   2 lessons

AIMS   **Linguistic:** to practise speaking skills, to link actions and words.
                             Other: to encourage co-operation between the children, to
                             achieve a group or class product, to learn how to use a video
                             camera.

DESCRIPTION   The children prepare and make a video of a dialogue from their
                             coursebook.

MATERIALS	Video camera and tapes, video player, 'props'.
IN CLASS	**1** Present and practise a dialogue from the textbook in the normal way.
	2 Divide the children into groups and tell them that they are going to video the dialogue. Choose a director, actors, and scene-shifters.
	3 Tell them to decide how to organize the furniture, 'props', who goes in and out when, what gestures to use, and so on, as well as where the camera should be, and when to start and stop it. The director should co-ordinate who does what, and when.
	4 The actors practise the dialogue, including gestures, facial expressions, and coming on to and off the 'set' at the right time.
	5 When everyone is ready, film the scene.
	6 Show the videos to the whole class.
FOLLOW-UP	Do one of the feedback activities from the Introduction.
COMMENTS	If you teach older children too, ask them to film scenes from the younger children's books. This provides material for the younger classes, and a real audience for the older children's work.

Acknowledgement

I would like to thank Amaya Arribi, Susi Diaz, and Elena de la Iglesia, who showed me just how motivating and useful making videos can be.

10 Putting it all together

Teachers have many roles in the classroom: two of the most important are planning lessons and organizing the classroom in a way that facilitates learning.

Here are some general ideas on organizing the classroom and planning lessons.

Classroom management

The atmosphere of the classroom, the attitude of the teacher, and the organization of the lesson all affect children's learning.

In the classroom itself

Try and achieve a warm, friendly, relaxed atmosphere.

Make sure that the chairs and tables are appropriately placed.

Make sure there is enough light and heating/ventilation.

Have a place where the children keep their English books and notebooks.

If at all possible create an 'English corner' for English reading books and worksheets for early finishers.

Display the children's work and relevant posters on the walls, and keep the displays up to date.

In the lessons

Create routines that the children recognize. Although they take time to explain and to establish, routines make the children feel secure and save a lot of time and explanation in the long run.

Mark the beginning of the lesson, for example with a song, by correcting homework, or with a brief recall of the previous lesson.

The 'core' of the lesson will vary, but always start by telling the children what activities they are going to do and, with older children, what the activities are for.

Mark the stages of the lesson clearly so that the children know when one activity finishes and another starts.

Give clear instructions for each activity and check that the children have understood by asking questions, or demonstrating the activity.

Make sure that the children know how long they can spend on an activity, and try and keep to the time limit as much as possible (though flexibility is a virtue too!).

Establish a signal or routine for finishing activities, for example clapping your hands twice and saying *Time to stop*.

Use as much English as you can (see Introduction) and make sure the children know when their first language is allowed and when not.

If the children are working in pairs or groups, walk around the classroom making comments, praising, and encouraging. You can take the opportunity to talk about their work in English: for example, *What's this? What colour is it? Who's this? What's he doing?*

Have something for the early finishers to do, for example an extra worksheet with a wordgame or puzzle, or perhaps they could go to the readers corner, or play with a game they have made in a previous lesson.

If you are doing a 'messy activity', leave enough time to clear up, and make sure that the children know they are responsible for tidying up the classroom. You might like to appoint different children to be responsible for pencils, colours, scissors, etc., or you may prefer each child to be responsible for his or her own table or workspace.

Ending a lesson well is as important as starting it well: it is often a good idea to end with a whole class activity such as a chant, a song, or a quick game. Alternatively, you can ask the children what they have done and what they have learned (see 'Feedback', page 11).

Try and keep a record of each child's progress—this can be a simple table on which you tick such things as the child's attitude to English, to classmates, achievement of tasks, and proficiency in the four skills. This will allow you to identify and hopefully resolve potential problems, and will certainly help when you are called on to evaluate the child.

Lesson content

The content of a lesson depends a great deal on the character of the class you are teaching and on their age and level. Here are some useful general points:

The younger the child, the shorter the attention span, so plan a series of activities per lesson: some quiet, some active, some involving the whole class, some in pairs or groups. These changes of pace and focus help keep the children interested and motivated.

Start the lesson with a 'warmer' that recalls the language of previous lessons and in some way connects with the content of the present lesson. In general, it is best to present new language in the first part of the lesson, then work on it, and dedicate the last part of the lesson to quieter, individual activities.

If you are presenting new vocabulary, use *structures* the children already know. If you are presenting new structures, use *vocabulary* that they know.

Remember to make the language as communicative and as relevant to the children as possible.

A balance of skills work, grammar, and vocabulary is as necessary as a balance of types of activity. Lessons with younger children should be based mostly on listening and speaking, while those with older children can contain a mix of skills.

Recycle language and vocabulary as much as possible: in different contexts, in different activities, and using different skills.

Build feedback activities into your lesson plans—this allows the children to have a say in the teaching/learning process, and will in turn help you to prepare more appropriate classes. See the Introduction for ideas on how to conduct feedback.

Lesson planning

Always be clear about your aims and choose activities that will help you and the children achieve them. Three approaches are outlined below:

1   Starting with the language

Decide which language point to focus on. Then think of topics that use this kind of language. For example, if you are working on *There is, there are*, a suitable topic could be 'Our school' or 'Our classroom'; if you are working on first conditionals, you could use 'Superstitions' as the topic. Plan a series of activities that present and practise the language, and that include the skills you want your children to acquire.

Example

Language point: *Has got* for possession—in affirmative, negative, and question form.

Possible topics:	The family, toys, descriptions of people/animals, illnesses.
Chosen topic:	Descriptions of people/animals/monsters.
Activities:	Present the parts of the body using yourself as a model.
	Play 'Teacher says' (see 1.1, 'Listen and do').
	Sing one of the 'Parts of the body' songs in 7.1, 'Action songs'.
	Put up flashcards of different people, and use them to introduce and practise *She's got/He hasn't got* (see 5.1, 'Flashcard ideas').
	Describe a person for the children to identify.
	Children describe and identify people in pairs (see 2.1, 'Simple speaking activities').
	Do a picture dictation of a monster (see 1.8, 'In the playground', for technique).
	Do 8.6, 'Twin plasticine monsters'.
	Make a monster catalogue using any of the techniques outlined in 8.10, 'Making books'.
	Play 'Happy families' (6.4).

2 Starting with a topic

Decide which topic you want to work on with your children, list the language points it suggests, and choose ones which are suitable for your group. Find activities which present and practise this language and which develop the children's language skills.

Example

General topic:	Food
Related topics:	Buying food, choosing from a menu, cooking, a healthy diet, food around the world, food and festivals/celebrations.
Language:	*I like/don't like, I'd like, Can I have ...?, Have you got ...?, Is/are there, You should/shouldn't, We/they eat*, food vocabulary.
Chosen topic:	Buying food, cooking.
Activities:	Present food vocabulary using flashcards (5.1) or a vocabulary network (5.2).

The children bring in food labels to make a poster.

Use the labels to practise *Can I have* and *I'd like some/a.*

Do a 'Find the differences' activity with a food cupboard to practise *Is there/Are there* (using the technique described in 2.2, 'On the farm').

Do a shopping role play, if possible using empty food packets.

Tell the story of 'Timmy goes shopping' (1.3).

Do 3.6, 'Making milkshakes'.

The children write their own simple recipes and make a class recipe book (see 8.10, 'Making books').

Do 3.5, 'At a restaurant'.

The children do a restaurant role play.

Do 'A questionnaire on health' (2.6).

3 Supplement the coursebook

Most teachers have a textbook to follow, and this not only saves you a lot of work, but also helps ensure that a balanced syllabus is covered. However, a textbook may not cover your children's needs exactly, and it is usually necessary to supplement it with other related activities. Also, a rest from the textbook provides a welcome change of pace for both yourself and the children.

Examples

In the book	*Supplementary activity*
Colours, numbers, letters:	1.4, 'Complete a grid'
	6.8, 'Body writing'
	7.1, 'Action songs': Ten little fingers
Parts of the body:	7.1, 'Action songs': Heads and shoulders, The hokey cokey
	8.6, 'Twin plasticine monsters'
Present simple for habits:	2.6, 'A questionnaire on health' 7.1, 'Action songs': Here we go round the mulberry bush
Present continuous:	2.2, 'On the farm'
The weather:	8.4, 'Make a weather clock'

Prepositions:	1.5, 'The Pied Piper'
	5.6, 'The lost pet'
Must, mustn't (obligation):	5.7, 'Keeping the rules'
At the end of a unit:	6.6, 'Carolyn's grammar game'
	6.3, 'Word games'.

Most of the activities in this book provide ideas for follow-up, linking different activities, and variations to help you adapt them to suit your children. The Index at the back of the book will help you to find activities on particular topics or language.

You can use many of the other activities in this book, such as 8.10, 'Making books', 6.7, 'A treasure hunt', or the songs and stories, to recycle language, to practise skills, or simply to do something different before going on to the next unit of your coursebook.

1

2

3

4

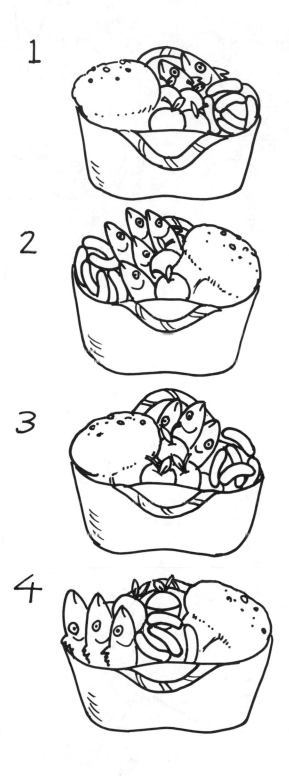

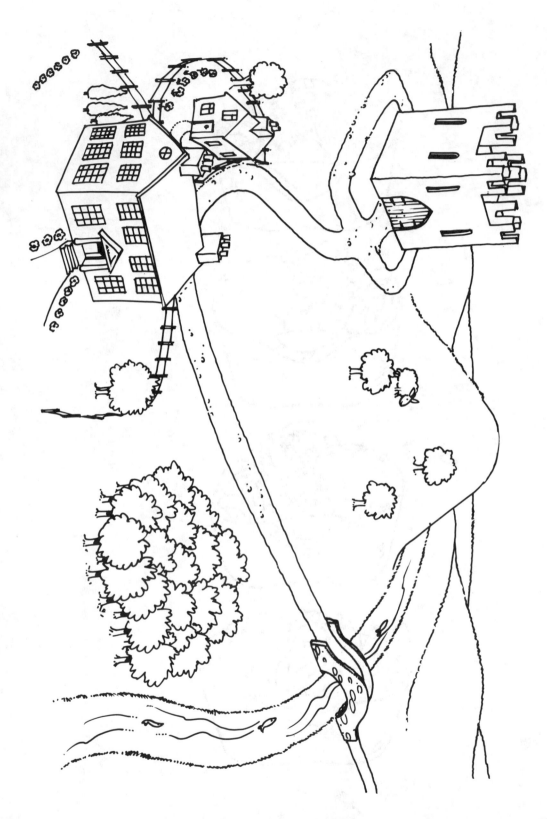

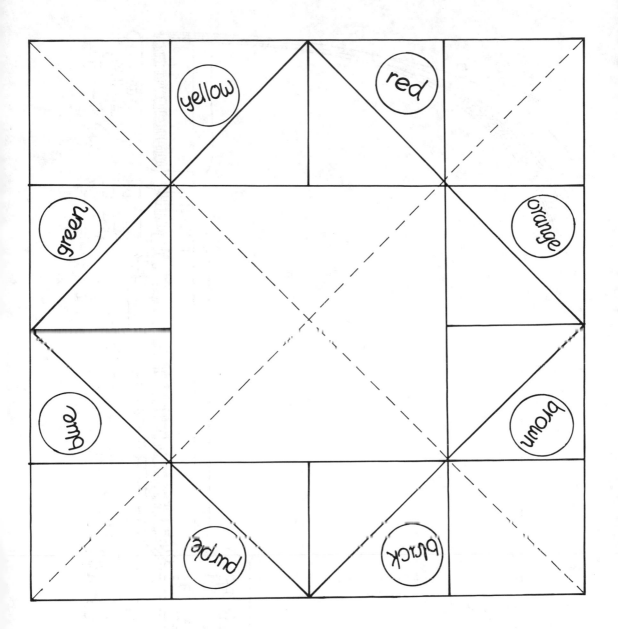

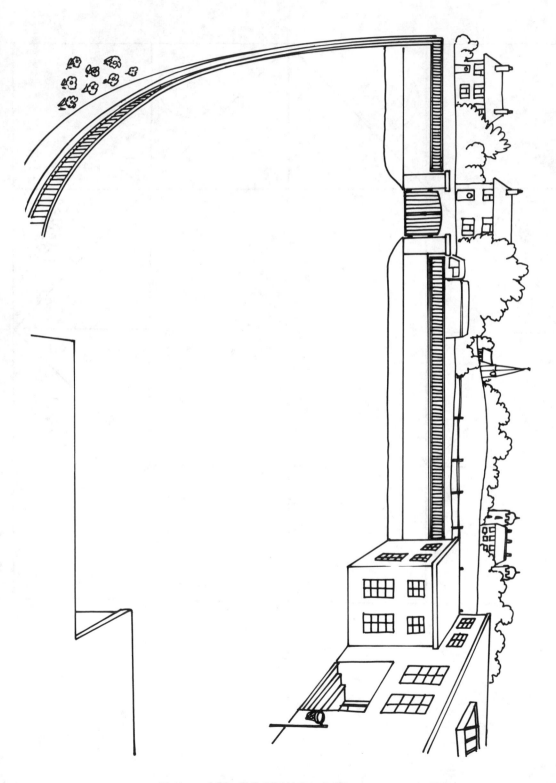

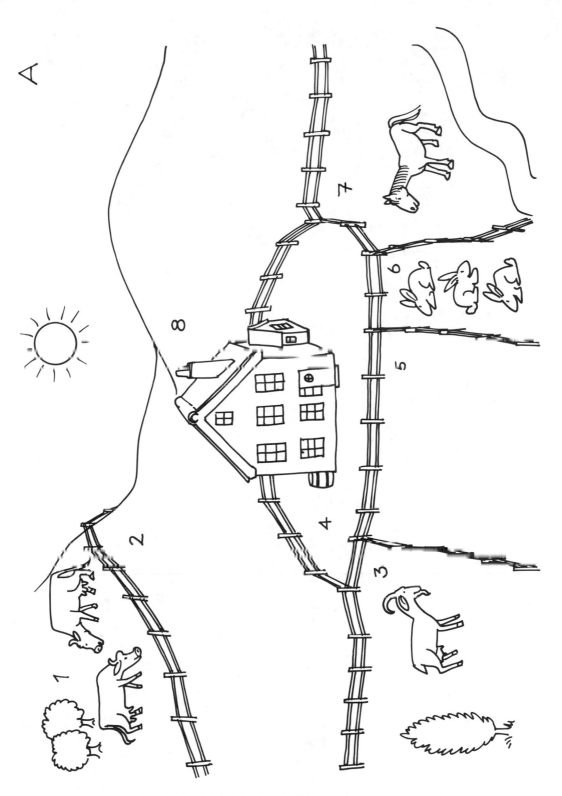

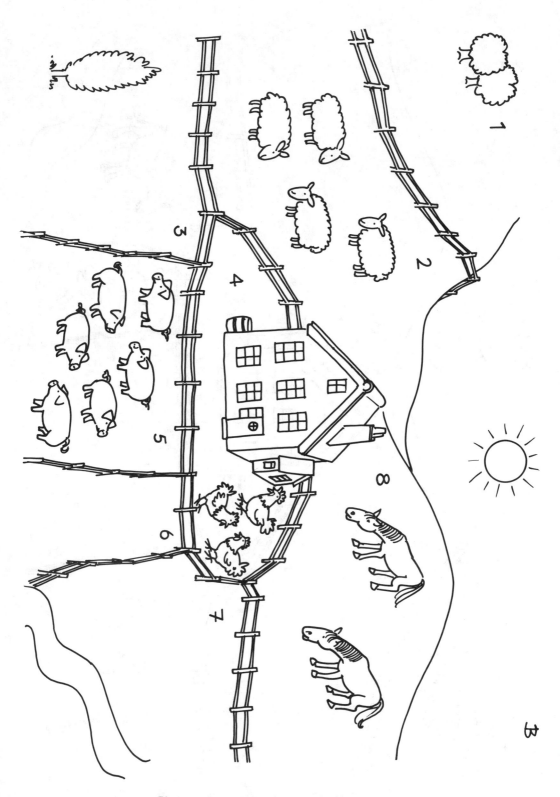

Are you healthy?

How often do you:

1   ... do exercise?
    A   Less than an hour a day
    B   Five hours a week
    C   More than five hours a week

2   ... sleep?
    A   Less than five hours a night
    B   Seven hours a night
    C   Ten hours a night

3   ... watch TV?
    A   More than four hours a day
    B   Two hours a day
    C   An hour a day

4   ... eat cakes, biscuits, and sweets?
    A   Six times a day
    B   Three times a day
    C   Less than once a day

5   ... eat fresh fruit and vegetables?
    A   Never
    B   Once a week
    C   Every day

6   ... clean your teeth?
    A   Never
    B   Three times a week
    C   Twice a day

SCORE

Count how many As, Bs, and Cs you have.

Mostly As:

You are not very healthy at all. You need to do more exercise, watch less television, and eat better food. Think about it!

Mostly Bs:

Not bad, but you can do a lot to improve your health. Think about what you eat and the exercise you do and try to improve!

Mostly Cs:

You are a very, very healthy person. Congratulations!

Secret file on 003

Age: _26_   Place of birth: _Istanbul, Turkey_

Lives in: _Edinburgh, Scotland_

Mother: _Famous writer of cookery books_   Father: _Mechanic_

Education: _Primary school in Istanbul, Secondary school in Madrid, University in Paris_

Languages: _English, Turkish, Spanish, French, Hungarian, Polish, Japanese_

Job: _Spy - pretends to be an English teacher_

Married? _No_

Pets: _Small alligator - eats fish_

Hobbies: _Fishing, making model railways_

Secret file on 004

Age: _____   Place of birth: _____

Lives in: _____

Mother: _____   Father: _____

Education: _____

Languages: _____

Job: _____

Married? _____

Pets: _____

Hobbies: _____

1 Colour the mouse's head brown.

2 Colour his tail brown too.

3 Colour his shirt green.

4 Colour his trousers red.

5 Draw flowers on the ends of the sticks in the mouse's hand.
   Colour them yellow, orange, red, blue, and pink.

6 Draw the sun in the sky. Colour it yellow.

7 Cut out the picture and stick it on the front of your card.

The washing line

The person on the ground floor plays football.

Jane and Mary's school uniform is a blue skirt and white blouse.

The person on the top floor likes whales.

Dawn loves swimming.

The schoolgirls live on the second floor.

Bob plays number nine in his local football team.

Peter's hobby is karate.

Dawn lives below Jane and Mary.

Anne's flat is on the top floor.

Peter lives on the third floor.

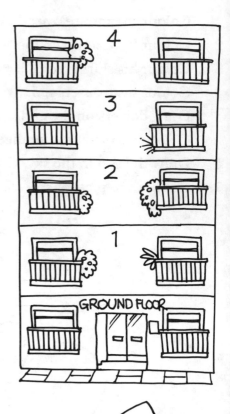

1. Devi and the tree

2. The thieves

Five hundred years ago, a young girl called Devi lived in a town in the mountains in India.

Taffy was a thief.

Her family's house had a big garden.

Sometimes Devi and her friends had picnics or played games together there.

Jake was a thief, too.

One day Jake saw some pictures in the newspaper.

'There are some diamonds in one of the rooms of the big house on the hill,' Jake said

Sometimes she sat and read her book under the trees.

'Let's go to the house tomorrow night. Let's steal the diamonds!'

There were some beautiful trees in the garden, but one was Devi's special tree.

'Good idea!' said Taffy. 'We're going to be rich!'

(From *Start Reading 4*, Derek Strange, OUP 1989)

At a restaurant

Read this dialogue, look at the menu, and work out the customers' bill.

Waiter	Good morning.
Children	Hello, can we have the menu, please?
Waiter	Yes, here you are.
Peter	Can I have a hamburger and chips with extra chips, please?
Jane	And I'd like a ham and mushroom pizza with extra olives, please.
Anna	And I want fish and chips and a salad, please.
Waiter	Anything to drink?
Peter	Orange juice, please.
Jane	Me too.
Anna	A Coke, please.
Waiter	Large, medium, or small?
Anna	Large, please.
(Later)	
Waiter	Would you like a dessert?
Peter	I'd like a banana split, please.
Jane	Can I have some chocolate cake, please?
Anna	Nothing for me, thanks.
(Later)	
Waiter	Here's your bill.

Menu

Main Courses

Soup	£1.75
Hamburger and chips	£2.50
Fish and chips	£3.25
Steak and chips	£4.50
Sausage and beans	£2.50
Steak and salad	£3.75

Pizzas

Cheese and tomato	£4.00
Ham and tomato	£4.50
Ham and mushroom	£4.25
Extra olives	£0.60
Salad	£1.75
Extra chips	£0.90

Drinks

Coke	
Large	£0.90
Medium	£0.75
Small	£0.65
Orange juice	£0.90
Coffee	£0.80

Desserts

Cheesecake	£1.80
Chocolate cake	£1.60
Ice cream	£1.20
Banana split	£2.00
Fresh fruit	£0.70

Shopping lists

Read the questions and then look at the lists and find the answers.

a. Which is the longest list?
b. Which is the shortest list?
c. Which lists have ice cream on them?
d. Which lists have bananas on them?
e. Which lists have sugar on them?
f. Which lists have coffee on them?
g. Which lists have chocolate powder on them?
h. Which lists have milk on them?

1
bananas
potatoes
milk
sugar
ice cream

2
milk
chocolate
    powder
biscuits
ice cream
butter

3
milk
apples
ice cream

chocolate
    powder

4
bananas
yoghurt
coffee
    powder
butter

5
coffee
    powder
biscuits
ice cream
sugar
milk

Recipes

Banana milkshake

1 banana
1 cup of milk
ice cream

1. Put two spoons of ice cream in the jar.
2. Mash the banana with a fork.
3. Put it in the jar with the ice cream and stir.
4. Add the milk.
5. Put the lid on the jar.
6. Shake it all together.
7. Pour it into a glass.

Chocolate milkshake

2 teaspoons of chocolate
   powder
1 teaspoon of hot water
1 glass of milk
ice cream

1. Put the chocolate powder into the jar.
2. Add the hot water and stir.
3. Add the milk and stir.
4. Add the ice cream.
5. Put the lid on the jar.
4. Shake it all together.
5. Pour it into a glass.

Coffee milkshake

1 teaspoon of coffee powder
1 glass of milk
ice cream
1 teaspoon of hot water
1 teaspoon of sugar

1. Put the coffee powder into the jar.
2. Add the hot water and stir.
3. Add the sugar.
4. Add the milk. Stir.
5. Add the ice cream.
6. Put the lid on.
7. Shake it all together.

Your lucky number

Read the instructions and find out your lucky number.

1 How old are you? Write the number in the triangle.
2 What's the date today? Write the number of the day in the circle.
3 How many children are there in your class? Write the number in the square.
4 How many letters are there in your name? Write the number in the rectangle.
5 Add up all the numbers. Write the total in the small circles: one number in each circle.
6 Add up the numbers in the small circles. Write the total in the star. This is your lucky number!

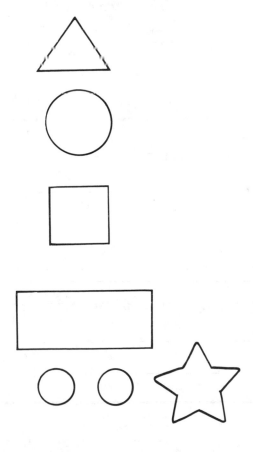

The other day ...

The other day I went to _____

There I saw a _____

So I said, _____

It said, 'You can have a wish.' This is what I wished for: _____

_____

_____

But when my wish came true, it wasn't exactly what I wanted! Instead,

_____

_____

Then I went home and my Mum and Dad said to me:

_____

_____

WORKSHEET 6.4A

Photocopiable © Oxford University Press

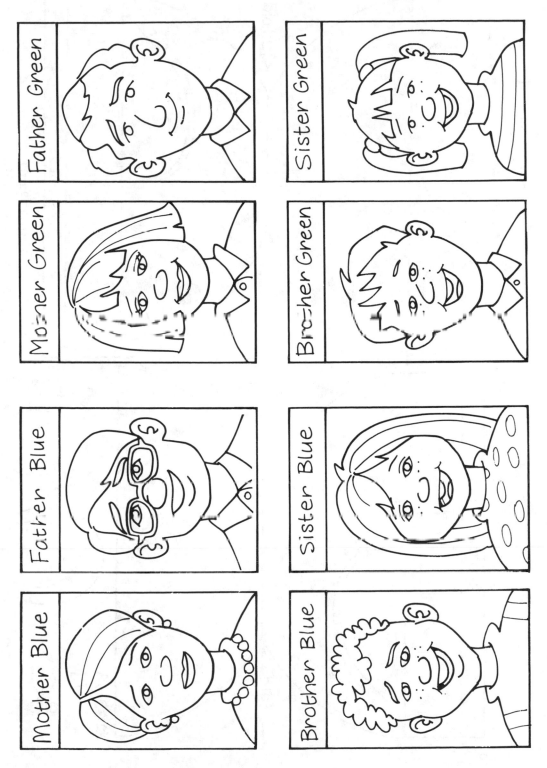

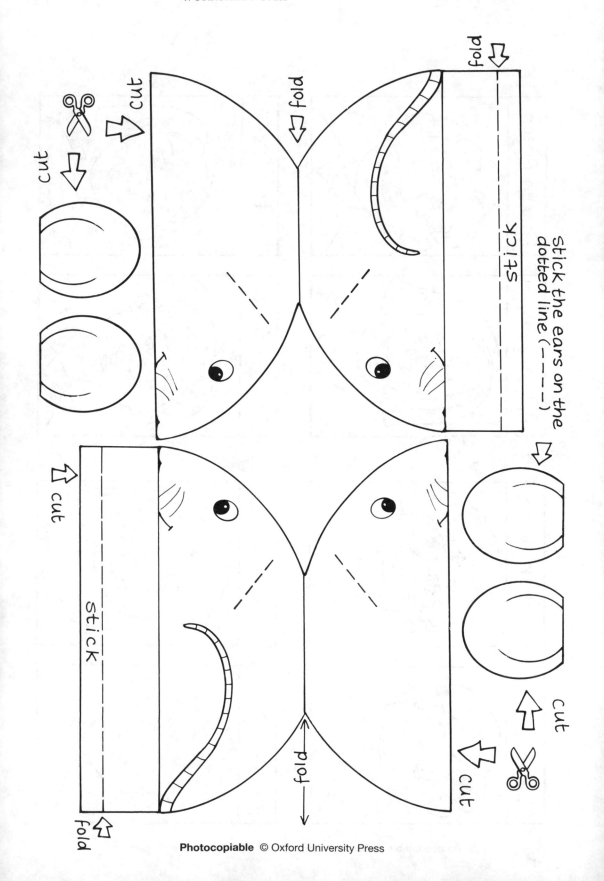

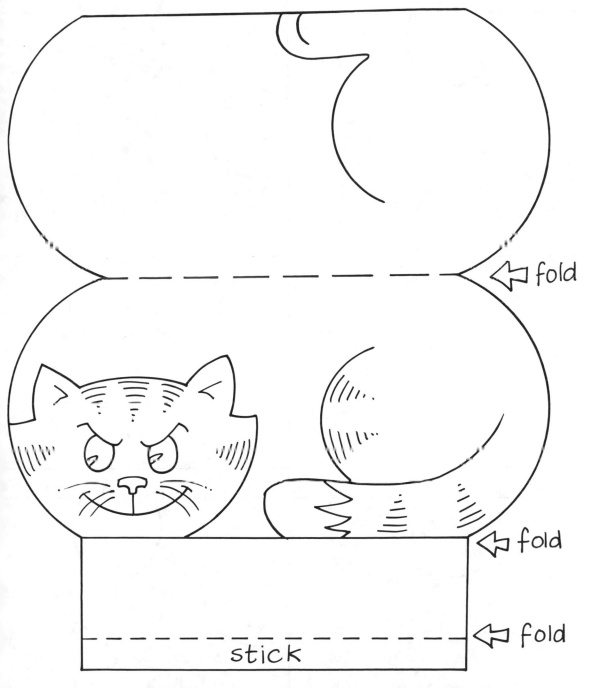

fold

fold

fold

stick

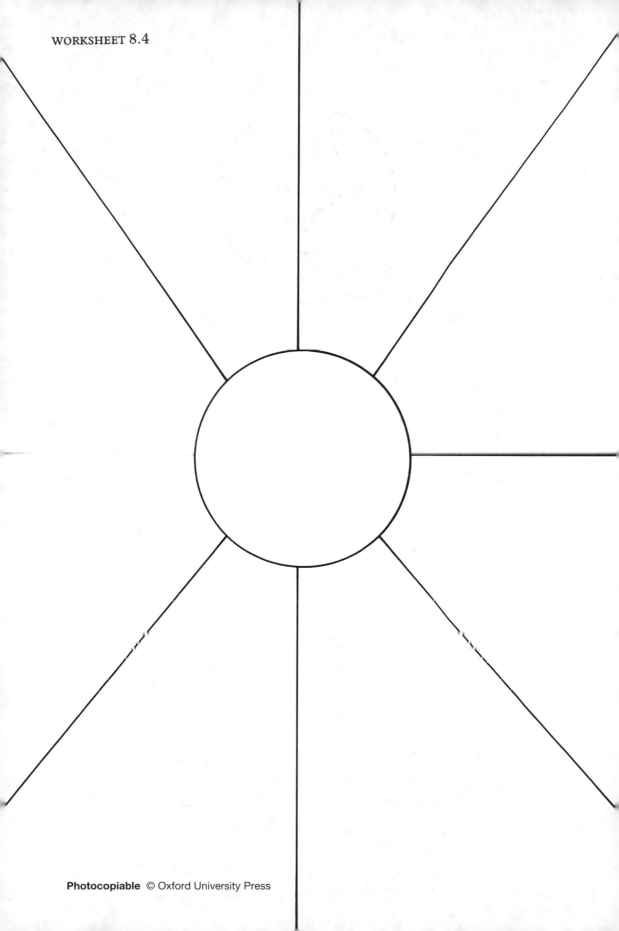

Growing seeds: Instructions

Day 1

1 Look carefully at your seed.
Draw a picture of it here.

2 Now put some water in your jam jar.
3 Put the seeds in the water and leave them for 24 hours.

Day 2

1 Draw a picture of your seeds here.
Are they different now?

2 Now tip the water out of the jar.
3 Cut some blotting paper and make it fit your jar, like in the picture.
4 Put about 5 cm of water in the jar.
5 Now carefully put your seeds between the blotting paper and the glass.
6 Now draw a picture of your jar.

7 Finally put your jar by the window. Don't forget to put your name on your jar.

Days 3, 4, 5, 6, etc.

1 Look at your seed every day.
2 Make sure it always has about 5 cm of water.
3 When you see a change, fill in the record sheet carefully.
4 Don't forget to measure your plant.

Growing seeds: record sheet

Date	How many days?	What does your plant look like? Draw a picture of your plant.	How tall is it?

Further reading

Many coursebook series for primary children now include packs of flashcards, posters, and song cassettes, as well as very useful teacher's notes, and often other supplementary material such as readers. Rather than list them all here, I would advise teachers to look through what is available carefully before making a choice.

Background reading

Theory

Brewster, J., G. Ellis, and **D. Girard**. 1992. *The Primary English Teacher's Guide*. Harmondsworth: Penguin. Examines the development of language teaching to young children, provides an analysis of teaching techniques and learning strategies, gives practical suggestions, and lists resources available.

British Council. 1985. *The Younger Learner: Bologna 1985*. London: Macmillan. One of the earliest collections of papers concerned with teaching English to primary children. Examines issues that are still relevant today.

Brumfit, C., J. Moon, and **R. Tongue** (eds.). 1991. *Teaching English to Children: From Practice to Principle*. London: Nelson. The first section describes some practical experiences in the primary language classroom, and the second gives some theoretical background.

Cullingford, C. 1990. *The Nature of Learning*. London: Cassell. Explores the holistic nature of human learning from an educational point of view.

Donaldson, M. 1978. *Children's Minds*. London: Fontana. A fascinating discussion of how children think and learn.

Lightbown, P. M. and **N. Spada.** 1993. *How Languages are Learned*. Oxford: Oxford University Press. An extremely useful, easy to read introduction to second language acquisition. Although the focus is mainly on adult learners, there is some discussion of children learning a second lanuguage and the book is of interest to anyone involved in language teaching.

Wells, G. 1987. *The Meaning Makers: Children Learning Language and Using Language to Learn*. London: Hodder and Stoughton. A fascinating account of a longitudinal study of English children learning their own language. Although not directly concerned with learning a second language, this book gives some interesting insights into the construction of meaning by children.

Wood, D. 1988. *How Children Think and Learn: The Social Contexts of Cognitive Development*. Oxford: Blackwell. Examines the major theories of cognitive development and considers their contribution to the classroom.

In the classroom

Asher, J. 1965. *Learning Another Language through Actions: The Complete Teacher's Guide*. Los Gatos, Ca: Sky Oaks Publications. Total Physical Response activities.

Dunn, O. 1983. *Beginning English with Young Children*. London: Macmillan.

Dunn, O. 1984. *Developing English with Young Children*. London: Macmillan. These two books examine the teaching of English to young learners and give practical solutions to common problems.

Halliwell, S. 1992. *Teaching English in the Primary Classroom*. Harlow: Longman. An introduction to teaching children English which raises key issues as well as giving practical advice to teachers.

Hutchinson, T. 1991. *Introduction to Project Work*. Oxford: Oxford University Press. A useful introduction to techniques which can be adapted for young learners.

Hutchinson, T. 1992. *Hotline*. Oxford: Oxford University Press. A secondary coursebook, but which includes useful suggestions for feedback activities.

Palim, J. and **P. Power.** 1990. *Jamboree*. London: Nelson. A book of activities to use with children, with photocopiable worksheets.

Reilly, V. and **S. M. Ward.** 1997. *Very Young Learners*. Oxford: Oxford University Press. 'Resource Books for Teachers' series. Ideas and guidance for teaching English to 3–6-year-olds.

Scott, W. and **L. H. Ytreberg.** 1990. *Teaching English to Children*. Harlow: Longman. A handbook for teachers which examines some of the issues and gives some ideas for practical activities.

Vale, D. with **A. Feunteun.** 1995. *Teaching Children English*. Cambridge: Cambridge University Press. A training course for teachers of young children in two parts: the first deals with methodology and classroom practice, while the second contains notes for teacher trainers. There is also a resource file.

Whiteford, R. and **J. Fitzsimmons.** 1988. *Bright Ideas Display*. Leamington Spa: Scholastic Publications. The 'Bright Ideas' series is written for primary teachers in England. The books cover a wide range of topics and activity types and are an excellent source of ideas.

Wright, A. 1984. *1000 Pictures for Teachers to Copy*. London: Nelson. An indispensable book of simple, easy-to-copy pictures, organized by theme and grammatically, to use when making flashcards and worksheets or when drawing on the board. He also gives advice for those of us who 'can't draw'.

Wright, A. 1989. *Pictures for Language Learning*. Cambridge: Cambridge University Press. Lots of ideas on how to use pictures in the classroom as well as where to find them and how to store them.

Listening

Davis, P. and **M. Rinvolucri.** 1989. *Dictation: New Methods, New Possibilities*. Cambridge: Cambridge University Press. New ideas for dictations, many of which can be adapted for the primary classroom.

Ur, P. 1984. *Teaching Listening Comprehension*. Cambridge: Cambridge University Press. A useful introduction to teaching the skill of listening. Although the activities are directed at older learners, the techniques can be adapted for primary classes.

Storytelling

See also Reading, below

Ahlberg, J. and **A. Ahlberg.** 1982. *Funnybones*. London: HarperCollins. A series of stories for native-speaker children about a family of skeletons. Includes 'In a dark, dark ...' (see 7.2).

Biro, V. 1985. *The Pied Piper of Hamelin*. Oxford: Oxford University Press.

Biro, V. 1985. *The Three Little Pigs*. Oxford: Oxford University Press. Traditional stories retold for young native speakers, with colourful illustrations.

Carle, E. 1974. *The Very Hungry Caterpillar*. London: Penguin. A popular story for young native-speaker children. Bilingual editions are available in several languages.

Ellis, G. and **J. Brewster.** 1991. *The Storytelling Handbook for Primary Teachers*. Harmondsworth: Penguin English. A very useful book full of ideas for using authentic story books with young learners.

Emblen, V. and **H. Schmitz.** 1991. *Learning through Story*. 'Bright Ideas' series. Leamington Spa: Scholastic Publications. A useful source of ideas on using stories in class.

Garvie, E. 1990. *Story as Vehicle: Teaching English to Young Children*. Clevedon/Philadelphia: Multilingual Matters. Includes some background theory on teaching children.

Hill, E. 1980. *Where's Spot?* London: Penguin. A popular children's book about a dog, which practises simple structures, and is available in many languages. There are several 'Spot' books, including 'word books' and 'learning to count' books.

Morgan, J. and **M. Rinvolucri.** 1983. *Once Upon a Time: Using Stories in the Language Classroom*. Cambridge: Cambridge University Press. Inspiration for using stories. Mostly for older and more advanced learners but the techniques can be adapted for primary use.

Nicoll, H. and **J. Pienkowski.** 1972. *Meg and Mog*. London: Penguin. A series of stories about a witch and her cat, for young native-speaker children.

The Piper of Hamelin. 1972. Oxford: Oxford University Press. 'Oxford Junior Graded Readers'. A retelling of the traditional story for young learners, at 750 headword level. Includes a glossary and exercises.

Wright, A. 1995. *Storytelling with Children*. Oxford: Oxford University Press. 'Resource Books for Teachers' series. Original ideas for using stories to teach English to children.

Wright, A. 1997. *Creating Stories with Children*. Oxford: Oxford University Press. 'Resource Books for Teachers' series. Shows how to help children invent and write their own stories in English.

Speaking

Hadfield, J. 1987. *Elementary Communication Games*. London: Nelson. A highly practical book with ideas and materials for communication activities with photocopiable masters.

Maley, A. and **A. Duff.** 1978. *Drama Techniques in Language Learning: A Resource Book of Communicative Activities for Language Teachers*. Cambridge: Cambridge University Press. A rich source of ideas with a dramatic flavour, many of which can be used with or adapted for young learners.

Reading

See also Storytelling (under Listening), above.

Ahlberg, A. and **J. Ahlberg.** The 'Happy Families' series. London: Penguin. An excellent series for young readers, based on the card game (see 6.4).

English Today Readers, Spellbinders, Start with English Readers. Oxford: Oxford University Press. Three series of graded readers for primary learners of English, including dictionaries and cassettes.

Greenwood, J. 1988. *Class Readers*. Oxford: Oxford University Press. 'Resource Books for Teachers' series. Practical advice and suggestions on using graded readers in class. Includes activities for older children.

Stepping into English. Oxford: Oxford University Press.
   Traditional stories adapted for young learners.
Thomson, R. 1989. 'Match This!' series: *Clothes, Body Bits,
   Food*. London: Franklin Watts. Books with split pages: riddles
   on one half, photographs with vocabulary on the other. The
   reader has to find which picture matches which text.
   Designed for native speakers, but the language is simple.
Tyler, J. 1981. *Usborne Book of World Geography*. London:
   Usborne. A book full of fascinating information on
   geography in the widest sense. Usborne publishes a wide
   range of educational books.

Writing

Hadfield, C. and **J. Hadfield.** 1990. *Writing Games*. London:
   Nelson. A collection of ideas for writing activities aimed at
   the older learner, but some of the techniques can be
   transferred to the primary classroom.
Hadley, H. 1992. *Inspirations for Poetry*. Leamington Spa:
   Scholastic Publications. This book is for primary teachers in
   England: it contains some stimulating ideas for using poetry
   that can be transferred to the English Language class

Vocabulary and grammar

Burridge, S. 1986. *Start with Words and Pictures*. Oxford:
   Oxford University Press. An alphabetical picture dictionary
   which gives examples of how words are used.
Granger, C. and **T. Hicks.** 1978. 'Contact English' series.
   Oxford: Heinemann. Suggestions for stories to use when
   presenting and practising structures and functions.
Holderness, J. 1986. *Start with Words and Pictures Activity
   Book*. Oxford: Oxford University Press. Exercises to develop
   dictionary skills.
Oxford Picture Power Dictionary. 1996. Oxford. Oxford
   University Press. A topic-based dictionary with lively stories
   and humorous illustrations. A cassette and activity book are
   available, as well as a Spanish edition.
Rinvolucri, M. 1985. *Grammar Games*. Cambridge:
   Cambridge University Press. A number of ways to make
   grammar practice more exciting. Designed for older
   students, but several of the games can be adapted for
   younger learners.
Ur, P. 1988. *Grammar Practice Activities: A Practical Guide for
   Teachers*. Cambridge: Cambridge University Press. A
   practical book full of ideas for presenting and practising
   structures, with a useful introduction.
Vale, D. and **S. Mullaney.** 1996. *The Cambridge Picture
   Dictionary*. Cambridge: Cambridge University Press. An

attractive theme-based dictionary with accompanying project book that encourages children to relate the words to their own world. Project Book available.

Wajnryb, R. 1990. *Grammar Dictation*. Oxford: Oxford University Press. 'Resource Books for Teachers' series. Listening and text reconstruction exercises to encourage learners to understand how language works. The examples are aimed at secondary and adult learners, but the technique can be used with older primary learners.

Wright, A. 1985. *Collins Picture Dictionary for Young Learners*. London and Glasgow: Collins ELT. Dictionary, workbook, and cassette. A clearly illustrated book of pictures organized by theme. There are some suggestions for language games at the back. Also published in bilingual editions.

Games

Retter, C. and **N. Valls.** 1984. *Bonanza*. Harlow: Longman. 77 language games for children, including colour picture cards.

Songs and chants

Beall, P. and **S. Nipp.** 1979. *Wee Sing*. Price Stern Sloan, P.O. Box 21942, Los Angeles, CA 90021, USA. A series of songs, games, and finger plays for native-speaker children, with books of words and music as well as cassettes and activity books.

Byrne, J. and **A. Waugh.** 1982. *Jingle Bells*. Oxford: Oxford University Press. A collection of traditional songs for use with young learners of English. There is a cassette of all the songs.

Graham, C. 1978. *Jazz Chants*. New York: Oxford University Press. Teacher's book, workbook, and cassette. A collection of jazz chants which help learners acquire English stress, rhythm, and pronunciation, as well as focusing on structures and themes.

Graham, C. 1979. *Jazz Chants for Children*. New York: Oxford University Press. Teacher's book, workbook, and cassette. Like Jazz Chants, but written specifically for children.

Graham, C. 1988. *Jazz Chant Fairytales*. New York: Oxford University Press. Workbook, and cassette. Fairytales told in verse to a strong rhythm, suitable for children with several years of English as an extensive range of vocabulary and structures is used.

King, K. and **I. Beck.** 1985. *Oranges and Lemons*. Oxford: Oxford University Press. A book of songs for young children, including the music.

Matterson, E. (ed.) 1969. *This Little Puffin*. London: Penguin. An extensive collection of nursery rhymes and songs (with music) from which teachers can select suitable ones for their children.

Murphey, T. 1992. *Music and Song.* Oxford: Oxford University Press. 'Resource Books for Teachers' series. A book full of ideas for using music in the English classroom. There is a chapter on young learners, and the other activities can often be adapted.

Traverso, P. 1992. 'Writing rhymes with children'. *jet* Vol. 2, No. 3, Issue 6. This issue has a whole section on using songs to teach English. See Periodicals, below.

Ward, S. 1980. *Dippitydoo.* Harlow: Longman. Activity book, teacher's guide, cassette. A book of songs with actions for young children.

Williams, S. and **I. Beck.** 1983. *Round and Round the Garden.* Oxford: Oxford University Press. A book of finger plays and rhymes for young children, including the actions.

Winer, Y. 1986. *Of Frogs and Snails.* Twickenham, UK: Belair Publications. A book of finger plays and action rhymes. Includes music and actions.

Creative activities

Bawden, J. 1991. *101 Things to Make.* Hemel Hempstead: Simon and Schuster Young Books. Craft activities aimed at native-speaker 7-year-olds and up. Illustrated with brightly coloured photos.

Bryant, D. 1990. *Things to make: 5-year-olds.* London: Piccolo. Games, monsters, recipes, word games, and masks for ages 5 *and up.* Not too childish for older children.

Danby, M. 1990. *Let's Cook.* London: Piccolo. Includes hot and cold recipes. Aimed at native-speaker children but very simple language.

Davies, M. 1990. *Crafts through the Year for 4–7-year-olds.* London: Michael O'Mara Books. Art activities on seasonal themes. Aimed at native speakers.

Hale, K. 1985. *Some Crafty Things to Do.* Oxford: Oxfam Education. Crafts from around the world, batik, musical instruments, cooking, etc. Aimed at 11–14-year-olds, but most of the activities are suitable for younger children.

Hall, G. 1992. *Developing Science.* London: Letts. An excellent book of science activities for children.

Henley, C. 1992. *My First Nature Activity Book.* London: Hippo Scholastic. Includes cut-out card games, weather charts, and some cooking, on the theme of nature.

Nakata, A. 1988. *Origami. Books 1–5.* Heian International, P.O. Box 1013, Union City, CA 94587, USA. Simple instructions for folded paper toys, clearly illustrated in colour.

Richards, R. 1990. *An Early Start to Science.* Hemel Hempstead: Simon and Schuster Young Books. More science activities for children.

Richards, R. 1992. *101 Science Surprises.* Hemel Hempstead:

Simon and Schuster Young Books. Despite the title, this is a brightly illustrated book of paper-folding activities for 7-year-olds and up.

Robson, D. 1990. *Rainy Days: Puppets*. London: Franklin Watts. All kinds of puppets, aimed at native-speaker 7-year-olds and up. Colour photos, fairly simple instructions.

Video

Cooper, R., M. Lavery, and **M. Rinvolucri,** 1991. *Video*. Oxford: Oxford University Press. 'Resource Books for Teachers' series. Gives practical ideas for video tasks and also has a section on making videos in the classroom.

Favourite Fairy Tales Video Series. Harlow: Longman. A collection of videos of the most famous of the Hans Christian Andersen fairy tales. There is an accompanying collection of illustrated books.

Muzzy in Gondoland. London: BBC English. Video course for young children. The material includes the video, audio cassette, activity booklets, workbooks, song books, readers, and teacher's/parents' notes.

Wizadora. Oxford: Oxford University Press. Eight amusing video episodes about a young wizard, designed to supplement primary coursebooks. The material includes the video, activity book, audio cassette, and teacher's guide.

Periodicals

jet (Junior English Teacher) magazine: unfortunately no longer published, but back issues are worth looking out for. It contains useful ideas for teaching English to children.

Click and *Crown*. Magazines written specially for young learners, with a cassette and a workbook, published six times a year. They provide a valuable source of material. Mary Glasgow Publications, 131–3 Holland Park Avenue, London W11 4UT, UK.

ELI Monthly Magazines. A 20-page, full colour magazine for teachers of primary children, also cartoon magazines *Ready* and *Let's Start!* for young learners. Midwest European Publications Inc., Subscription Services, 824 Noyes Street, Evanston, IL 60201, USA.

IATEFL Young Learners Special Interest Group organises conferences and publishes a magazine. For more information contact: IATEFL, 3 Kingsdown Chambers, Tankerton, Whitstable, Kent CT5 2DJ, England (World Wide Web http://www.man.ac.uk/IATEFL).

Other titles in the Resource Books for Teachers series

Beginners, by Peter Grundy—over 100 original, communicative activities for teaching both absolute and 'false' beginners, including both children and adults, as well as those who do not know the Latin alphabet. (ISBN 0 19 437200 6)

CALL, by David Hardisty and Scott Windeatt—a bank of practical activities, based on communicative methodology, which make use of a variety of computer programs. (ISBN 0 19 437105 0)

Class Readers, by Jean Greenwood—practical advice and activities to develop extensive and intensive reading skills, listening activities, oral tasks, and perceptive skills. (ISBN 0 19 437103 4)

Classroom Dynamics, by Jill Hadfield—a practical book to help teachers maintain a good working relationship with their classes, and so promote effective learning. (ISBN 0 19 437096 8)

Conversation by Rob Nolasco and Lois Arthur—more than 80 activities which develop students' ability to speak confidently and fluently. (ISBN 0 19 437096 8)

Creating Stories with Children, by Andrew Wright—original ideas for helping children to tell and write stories in English. Encourages creativity, confidence, and fluency and accuracy in spoken and written English. (ISBN 0 19 437204 9)

Cultural Awareness, by Barry Tomalin and Susan Stempleski— activities to challenge stereotypes, using cultural issues as a rich resource for language practice. (ISBN 0 19 437194 8)

Drama, by Charlyn Wessels—first-hand, practical advice on using drama to teach spoken communication skills and literature, and to make language learning more creative and enjoyable. (ISBN 0 19 437097 6)

Exam Classes, by Peter May—includes activities to help prepare for a wide variety of public examinations, including most of the main American and British exams such as TOEFL and the new UCLES exams. (ISBN 0 19 437208 1)

Grammar Dictation, by Ruth Wajnryb—also known as 'dictogloss', this technique improves students' understanding and use of grammar by reconstructing texts. (ISBN 0 19 437097 6)

Learner-based Teaching, by Colin Campbell and Hanna Kryszewska—over 70 language practice activities which unlock the wealth of knowledge that learners bring to the classroom. (ISBN 0 19 437163 8)

Letters, by Nicky Burbidge, Peta Gray, Sheila Levy, and Mario Rinvolucri—demonstrates the rich possibilities of letters for language and cultural study. Contains numerous photocopiables and a section on email. (ISBN 0 19 442149 X)

Literature, by Alan Maley and Alan Duff—an innovatory book on using literature for language practice. (ISBN 0 19 437094 1)

Music and Song, by Tim Murphey—shows teachers how 'tuning in' to their students' musical tastes can increase motivation and tap a rich vein of resources. (ISBN 0 19 437055 0)

Newspapers, by Peter Grundy—creative and original ideas for making effective use of newspapers in lessons. (ISBN 0 19 437192 6)

Project Work, by Diana L. Fried-Booth—practical resources to bridge the gap between the classroom and the outside world. (ISBN 0 19 437092 5)

Pronunciation, by Clement Laroy—imaginative activities to build confidence and improve all aspects of pronunciation. (ISBN 0 19 437089 9)

Role Play, by Gillian Porter Ladousse—from highly controlled conversations to improvised drama, and from simple dialogues to complex scenarios. (ISBN 0 19 437095 X)

Self-Access, by Susan Sheerin—helps teachers with the practicalities of setting up and managing self-access study facilities. (ISBN 0 19 437099 2)

Storytelling with Children, by Andrew Wright—thirty stories plus hundreds of exciting ideas for using any story to teach English to children aged 7 to 14. (ISBN 0 19 437202 2)

Translation, by Alan Duff—provides a wide variety of translation activities from many different subject areas. (ISBN 0 19 437104 2)

Very Young Learners, by Vanessa Reilly and Sheila M. Ward—advice and ideas for teaching children aged 3 to 6 years. Over 80 activities including games, songs, drama, stories, and art and crafts, and numerous photocopiable pages. (ISBN 0 19 437209 X)

Video, by Richard Cooper, Mike Lavery, and Mario Rinvolucri—video watching and making tasks involving the language of perception, observation, and argumentation. (ISBN 0 19 437192 6)

Vocabulary, by John Morgan and Mario Rinvolucri—a wide variety of communicative activities for teaching new words to learners of any foreign language. (ISBN 437091 7)

Writing, by Tricia Hedge—presents a wide range of writing tasks to improve learners' 'authoring' and 'crafting' skills, as well as guidance on student difficulties with writing. (ISBN 0 19 437098 4)

Indexes

Activities which can be adapted to practise various structures or vocabulary topics are not listed here. See, for example, 5.2, 'Vocabulary networks', 6.6, 'Carolyn's grammar game', or 8.10, 'Making books'.

See Chapters 1–4 for activities designed specifically to practise the four skills of listening, speaking, reading, and writing.